KAREN MONROE

Contents

PART THREE: *The General*

PART FOUR: *The Statesman*

CHAPTER FORTY-ONE

The Ruins of the Past

WHEN WASHINGTON CONSENTED IN 1783 to serve as first president of the Order of the Cincinnati, he imagined himself signing on to a fraternal organization that was charitable in intent and incontrovertibly good. So convinced was he of its virtue that he did not agonize over becoming president the way he mulled over comparable decisions in his life. Though not a founder of the group, he felt a fraternal camaraderie with his fellow officers and cottoned to the idea of perpetuating their comradeship. He even offered a five-hundred-dollar gift to invigorate the Cincinnati. Distracted by other matters, he didn't heed at first the rancorous debates brewing over the organization's character. "I was conscious that my own proceedings on that subject were immaculate," he later declared a shade defensively.[1] As shown by the slavery issue, Washington didn't wish to be ensnared in political controversy or do anything that might mar his hard-won image as the incarnation of national unity.

But the formation of a hereditary society, with membership inherited through eldest sons, awakened the hostility toward aristocracy bred by the Revolution. Blasted as elitist, the society raised the dread specter of a military caste that might dominate American political life. That Washington lacked a male heir spared him no criticism. After all, the society's very name paid tribute to his ineffable mystique. In hunting down monarchical plots, the new nation displayed an active, often paranoid imagination. In later years Jefferson stated that it had "always been believed" that some army officers, especially Steuben and Knox, had offered a crown to Washington and started the Cincinnati only when he rejected it, hoping the hereditary order would "be engrafted into the future frame of government and placing Washington still at the head."[2] There was no evidence whatsoever that Steuben and Knox ever contemplated such an offer.

When Benjamin Franklin's daughter transmitted to him press reports about the new society, he replied that he could understand the Chinese practice of honoring one's parents, who after all had achieved something. To honor descendants, however, merely from the accident of biology, was "not only groundless and absurd but often hurtful to that posterity." Any sort of hereditary society, he declared, would stand "in direct opposition to the solemnly declared sense" of the new country.[3] John Adams also went on the warpath against the Cincinnati, damning the group as "the deepest piece of cunning yet attempted . . . the first step taken to deface the beauty of our temple of liberty."[4]

No sooner had Washington announced the first national meeting, to be held in Philadelphia in May 1784, than he was taken aback by angry rumbles about the hereditary requirement, an early inkling of the boisterous democratic tendencies that would reshape the country and challenge the preeminence of the former officer corps. Henry Knox, the society's first secretary general, summed up this dissent for Washington: "The idea is that it has been created by a foreign influence in order to change our forms of government."[5] Even Lafayette in Paris, heading the French chapter, wound up embroiled in conflict: "Most of the Americans here are indecently violent against our association . . . [John] Jay, [John] Adams, and all the others warmly blame the army."[6] For Washington, it was a painful contretemps: his first public act since the war had backfired, and it engulfed him in a flaming controversy. Since the group's power derived largely from its identification with Washington, he lacked the option of staying aloof and remaining deaf to this rising storm of criticism.

Always jealous of his reputation for republican purity, Washington hated to have his integrity questioned. To defuse the controversy, he was eager to eliminate the group's more odious features. As he told Jonathan Trumbull, Jr., "If we cannot convince the people that their fears are ill-founded, we should (at least in a degree) yield to them and not suffer that which was intended for the best of purposes to produce a bad one which will be the consequence of divisions."[7] As was his wont, he responded to criticism by soliciting disparate opinions. He turned to Jefferson, who predictably faulted the group for relying on "preeminence by birth" and also worried that some future president of the Cincinnati might "adopt a more mistaken road to glory."[8]

By the time of the Philadelphia meeting, Washington was eager to respond to criticism swirling around the group. Some of it he thought maliciously exaggerated "by designing men to work their own purposes upon terrified imaginations," but he acknowledged the genuine kernel of discontent.[9] In his inaugural speech, he stated categorically that the Society of the Cincinnati must mend its ways. In notes prepared for the speech, he listed his reform agenda: "Strike out every word, sentence, and clause which has a political tendency. Discontinue the hereditary part in all its connections . . . Admit no more honorary members into the society. Reject subscriptions or donations from every person who is not a citizen of the United States."[10] Delivering this blunt message, the ordinarily circumspect Washington was fiery and outspoken. As one of those present, Winthrop Sargent, observed, "In a very long speech, and with much warmth and agitation, he expressed himself on all the parts of the institution deemed exceptionable and reiterated his determination to vacate his place in the society, if it could not be accommodated to the feeling and pleasure of the several states."[11]

Washington's performance in Philadelphia showed that he could be a forceful orator who spoke at length and with passion if he wanted to. That he often failed to do so was because he preferred to keep his own counsel and reveal only a tiny portion of his thoughts, keeping his options open. He knew his power before a crowd of people, as shown during the Newburgh uprising, and could turn on the spigot of his oratory at will. The speech also showed Washington's awareness of his unique political standing—and his willingness to exploit it by threatening to resign if objectionable traits of the Cincinnati were not removed. His emotional comments also suggest extreme irritation at being dragged into the unwelcome glare of public controversy. The methodical Washington didn't like to be taken by surprise. The French engineer Pierre-Charles L'Enfant had designed for the society an insignia with a bald eagle, hung from a pale blue and white ribbon. When French officers gave Washington this medal, adorned with diamonds and emeralds, he secreted it in a drawer and never wore it for fear of being branded a pseudoroyalist.

Although he agreed to serve a three-year term as president, he later said that it was "much against my inclination," a way to salve any wounded feelings among his fellow officers.[12] His success in purging the society of its disputed features was only partial. He wanted the group to discard national meetings and limit assemblies to state chapters, which, among other things, would lower his own high-profile connection with it. Openly opposing him, delegates voted to retain the general gatherings, and several state chapters refused to accept the alterations adopted at the national meeting, leaving the hereditary feature intact. If Washington had shown political agility in tackling the group's problems and juggling conflicting demands, he had also seen that he couldn't determine the final outcome and was reluctant to be party to something beyond his control.

Having quieted the uproar temporarily, Washington knew that "the jealousies of the people are rather asleep than removed on this occasion."[13] Had it not been for his deep sense of solidarity with American and French officers and a respect for the group's laudable work for widows and orphans, Washington probably would have severed his ties with the Cincinnati and proposed its abolition. The intransigence of state societies in contesting reforms only hardened his resolve to insulate himself from them. He devised a compromise whereby he remained a figurehead and signed official forms, while keeping a self-protective distance, planning all the while to step down as president before the next general meeting in 1787.

A far happier association was with the Masons. Whatever conspiracy theories later circulated about the group, the brotherhood provoked no suspicions in late-eighteenth-century America, and Washington seldom missed a chance to salute their lodges. The group's soaring language, universal optimism, and good fellowship appealed to him. When he was sent Masonic ornaments late in the war, he recast the struggle in Masonic imagery, saying that all praise was due "to the *Grand Architect* of the Universe, who did not see fit to suffer his superstructures and justice to be subjected to the ambition of the princes of this world."[14] In June 1784 he was inducted into the Alexandria lodge as an honorary member, which gave him dual membership there and in the Fredericksburg lodge. Later elevated to master of the Alexandria lodge, he earned the distinction of being the only Mason to hold this post while simultaneously serving as president of the United States. Where he had kept a wary attitude toward the Cincinnati, he proudly embraced Masonic rituals. When an elderly resident of Alexandria, William Ramsay, was buried in 1785, Washington noted in his diary that he had not only attended the funeral but "walked in procession as a free mason, Mr. Ramsay in his lifetime being one and now buried with the ceremonies and honors due to one."[15]

In 1785 Washington formed an institutional tie that led him ineluctably back into national politics. His western trip the previous autumn had rekindled his fervent faith in the Potomac River as the gateway to America's interior. After the trip he lobbied Virginia governor Benjamin Harrison to form a company that would make the Potomac, with its stony obstructions, waterfalls, and rapids, navigable to the headwaters of the Ohio. Completing the linkage would require additional canals, locks, and portages. However partial he was to the Potomac, Washington also held out the possibility of extending the James River. He pressed Madison and others in the Virginia House of Delegates to champion the navigation project, then took up the same cause with Maryland legislators in Annapolis. Since Virginia and Maryland shared rights to the Potomac, any project required the joint approval of both states. "It is now near 12 at night," an exhausted Washington wrote to Madison from Annapolis on December 28, "and I am writing with an aching head, having been constantly employed in this business since the 22nd without assistance from my colleagues."[16] Madison was agog at Washington's stamina. "The earnestness with which he espouses the undertaking is hardly to be described," he remarked to

Jefferson, "and shows that a mind like his, capable of grand views . . . cannot bear a vacancy."[17]

Washington's advocacy of the Potomac project united a private motivation (to enhance the wealth of western landowners such as himself) with a political motivation (to bind western settlers to the United States and forge a national identity). He was disturbed by ongoing clashes between settlers and Indians but thought it fruitless to try to stem the restless droves of immigrants pushing ever farther westward. Although the government couldn't halt this tide, it could guide it into constructive channels. "The spirit of emigration is great," he told Richard Henry Lee. "People have got impatient and tho[ugh] you cannot stop the road, it is yet in your power to mark the way."[18]

Washington became something of a monomaniac about the Potomac River project, and more than one Mount Vernon visitor was trapped in the talons of this obsession. When Elkanah Watson stayed there in January 1785, he described the inland navigation scheme as Washington's "constant and favorite theme."[19] Waving away questions about the Revolutionary War and dwelling compulsively on the river project, Washington computed the distances from Tidewater Virginia to spots in the interior. "Hearing little else for two days from the persuasive tongue of the great man," wrote Watson, "I confess completely infected me with the canal mania."[20]

In early January 1785 Virginia and Maryland decided to survey the two potential waterways to the Ohio Country and incorporated a pair of private companies, the Potomac River Company and the James River Company, to extend those rivers into the interior. To finance this extensive work, the legislatures would allow entrepreneurs to charge tolls on the waterways. Imagining that the companies would be quite lucrative, Washington had no qualms about businessmen booking large profits as long as their work served the public weal and provided a model for future government action.

While Washington rejoiced over his legislative victories, the state of Virginia threw him into a profound dilemma by deeding him a gift of fifty shares of Potomac River Company stock and one hundred shares of James River Company stock to recognize his services to the state. Having sacrificed a salary throughout the war, Washington was not about to accept payment now; nor did he want to seem vain or offend his fellow Virginians by brusquely dismissing their kind gesture. He admitted to Governor Harrison that "no circumstance has happened to me since I left the walks of public life, which has so much embarrassed me." If he spurned the gift, he feared, people would think "an ostentatious display of disinterestedness or public virtue was the source of the refusal." On the other hand, he wanted to remain free to articulate his views without arousing suspicions that "sinister motives had the smallest influence in the suggestion."[21] He valued his reputation for integrity, calling it "the principal thing which is laudable in my conduct."[22] Noting that such "gratuitous gifts are made in other countries," Washington wanted to establish a new benchmark for the behavior of public figures in America and eliminate petty or venal motives.[23]

Perplexed, Washington sent a flurry of letters to confidants, asking how to handle the unwanted gift. Beleaguered by money problems at Mount Vernon, he nevertheless tried to project the cavalier image of an affluent planter who had far more money than he needed. Throughout his life he cherished the pose of noblesse oblige in public service, even if he could scarcely afford it. Referring to his lack of children, he told Henry Knox airily, "I have nobody to provide for and I have enough to support me through life in the plain and easy style in which I mean to spend the remainder of my days."[24] In fact, Washington had insufficient money to support himself, his wards, and his slaves, and his style of life was scarcely plain and easy. He came up with an enlightened solution: he would hold the gift shares in trust for public education, possibly for the creation of "two charity schools, one on each river for the education and support of the children of the poor and indigent," especially those who had lost fathers in the war.[25] The final disposition of the money was deferred for many years.

To iron out differences between Virginia and Maryland over Potomac navigation, Washington presided over an interstate conference at Mount Vernon in 1785. He was also elected president of the Potomac River Company, for which he tirelessly proselytized. In early August he climbed into a canoe and undertook the first of his periodic inspection tours of the Potomac, investigating submerged obstacles at Seneca Falls and Shenandoah Falls by personally shooting the rapids. He was also involved in hiring a European superintendent and dozens of indentured servants to build the canals and locks. Soon teams of slaves went to work, their heads shaved to make it more difficult for them to escape without detection. Washington's ambition was huge: the lock canal constructed around Great Falls alone would rank as the biggest civil engineering project in eighteenth-century America. To carve open the interior, the Virginia legislature authorized the building of the Chesapeake and Ohio Canal, which would connect the Potomac and Ohio rivers, and the Kanawha Canal, linking the James with the Great Kanawha River in western Virginia. Both projects took decades to reach fruition.

A determined man, George Washington reveled in having overcome great skepticism to establish the Potomac River Company. When Robert Hunter visited Mount Vernon in November, he noticed that his host engaged in uncharacteristic gloating: "The general sent the bottle about pretty freely after dinner and gave 'Success to the navigation of the Potomac' for his toast, which he has very much [at] heart, and when finished will, I suppose, be the first river in the world . . . He is quite pleased at the idea of the Baltimore merchants laughing at him and saying it was a ridiculous plan and would never succeed."[26]

The plan to extend navigation of the Potomac influenced American history in ways that far transcended the narrow matter of commercial navigation. It created a set of practical problems that could be solved only by cooperation between Virginia and Maryland, setting a pattern for a seminal interstate conference at Annapolis in September 1786 and indeed the Constitutional Convention itself in 1787. Coordinating the efforts of two states confirmed Washington's continental perspective and sense of the irreparable harm that could be done by squabbling among states unconstrained by an effective national government. When Edward Savage painted *The Washington Family,* he shrewdly made the Potomac River, wending its way west in the background, a central element of the composition. Washington continued to tout the Potomac as "the great avenue into the western country . . . which promises to afford a capacious asylum for the poor and persecuted of the earth."[27] The Potomac River Company never lived up to these grandiose expectations: in the nineteenth century it went bankrupt, having penetrated no farther than Cumberland in the foothills of the Allegheny Mountains. But its real value in American politics had long since been realized.

FOR ALL THE HOPEFULNESS of his postwar life, Washington retained wistful recollections about his prewar existence, especially his relationship with George William and Sally Fairfax. Wartime duties had precluded him from acting as caretaker of Belvoir, and he was alarmed to hear rumors as early as 1778 that the estate was "verging fast to destruction."[28] Before the war the Fairfaxes had returned to England to follow a suit in Chancery, which involved a sizable estate left to George William by a relative; the case degenerated into a ghastly, never-ending Dickensian donnybrook. George William told Washington in August 1778 that the case was "as far from a conclusion as ever, owing to the villainy of my solicitor."[29] Lacking the income expected from the suit's resolution and deprived of any money from Virginia, the hitherto rich couple had to retrench drastically. They were both broken in health and had bought a small cottage near Bath so they could take the spa waters. There a chastened General John Burgoyne, after his Saratoga defeat, sought out the couple and hand-delivered a personal letter from General George Washington.

During the last year of the war, Belvoir had been severely damaged by fire, but for more than a year Washington could neither find the time nor muster the nerve to visit it. Then in late January 1785 he made a midwinter visit and grew awash in nostalgia. On February 27 he sent a heartfelt letter to George William in which he described the ravages visited upon their beloved Belvoir:

I took a ride there the other day to visit the ruins—and ruins indeed they are. The dwelling house and the two brick buildings in front underwent the ravages of the fire; the walls of which are very much injured. The other houses are sinking under the depredation of time and inattention and I believe are now scarcely worth repairing. In a word, the whole are, or very soon will be, a heap of ruin. When I viewed them—when I considered that the happiest moments of my life had been spent there—when I could not trace a room in the house (now all rubbish) that did not bring to my mind the recollection of pleasing scenes, I was obliged to fly from them and came home with painful sensations and sorrowing for the contrast.[30]

Whenever he gazed longingly toward Belvoir, he admitted, he wished that George William and Sally Fairfax would return to America and rebuild their residence while staying at Mount Vernon. He added that Martha joined him in this fervent wish.

This letter is remarkable in two ways. Washington states that the happiest moments of his life were spent not with his wife but with George William and Sally Fairfax, although one suspects he really had Sally in mind. Does the letter suggest that George William knew of the romantic liaison between his wife and Washington? Or does it tell us that their relationship was more an affectionate friendship than an adulterous affair, enabling Washington to refer to it with complete safety? Perhaps it confirms that Washington's fondness for Sally Fairfax had been a youthful dalliance that everyone now recognized as such. We will never know the full truth of this tantalizing but finally murky story. The letter is also notable in showing us how incurably sentimental Washington was beneath the surface—he could experience an eruption of memories so overpowering that he had to flee the scene.

In reply, George William Fairfax talked of the picturesque valley of dairy farms in which he and Sally lived and asserted they were too old to contemplate a return to America. Sally had pored over Washington's letter with great care, and his description of the ride to Belvoir had provoked an equally strong response in her. "Your pathetic description of the ruin of Belvoir House produced many tears and sighs from the former mistress of it," wrote George William—doubtless what Washington yearned to hear.[31] Sally volunteered to send Washington seeds for trees and shrubs for Mount Vernon, and he reacted with typical gallantry, reassuring George William that "while my attentions are bestowed on the nurture of [the seeds], it would, if anything was necessary to do it, remind me of the happy moments I have spent in conversations on this and other subjects with that lady at Belvoir."[32] So Washington again openly alluded to his special relationship with Sally Fairfax without fearing repercussions. After years of precarious health, George William Fairfax died on April 3, 1787. By that point the Constitutional Convention was looming, and Washington, sidetracked by political business, declined to act as American executor of his friend's estate.

The themes of love and marriage were often on Washington's mind after the war. Before it ended, Lund Washington had sounded him out on the prospective marriage of Jacky Custis's widow, Eleanor Calvert Custis, to Dr. David Stuart. Washington customarily refrained from giving advice in such situations because if he supported it, he might push a couple into an unwanted marriage, but if he opposed it, the young couple would blithely ignore him anyway. Nevertheless he went on to say that if Eleanor asked him, he would counsel her thus: "I wish you would make a prudent choice, to do which many considerations are necessary: such as the family and connections of the man, his fortune (which is not the *most* essential in my eye), the line of conduct he has observed, and disposition and frame of his mind. You should consider what prospect there is of his proving kind and affectionate to you; just, generous, and attentive to your children; and how far his connections will be agreeable to you."[33] Rather glaringly absent from this eminently reasonable list is romance—perhaps the sole ingredient lacking in Washington's otherwise happy, satisfying match with Martha. At the same time, he knew that genuine friendship formed the foundation of a marriage, and this, at the very least, he had found in abundance with his wife.

Martha viewed marriage in a similarly pragmatic light. When her niece Fanny contemplated marriage to George Augustine Washington, Martha tried to coach her in sizing up marital prospects. She recommended that Fanny look at a man's character and worldly prospects—whether he was honest, upright, hardworking, and likely to be a good provider. She didn't mention looks or charm or compatibility or any of the other romantic prerequisites that might preoccupy a modern woman.

When Fanny and George Augustine decided to get married, the Washingtons were jubilant about the match of these two young favorites. Before the October 1785 wedding, Washington paid for his nephew to spend time in the West Indies in an attempt to repair his health. Although the Washingtons invited the young couple to share the Mount Vernon mansion with them, the suggestion came loaded with one big caveat. As Washington told Lund, the young couple had been urged to "make this house their home till the squalling and trouble of children might become disagreeable."[34] By this point, the Washingtons had probably had their fill of the responsibility of caring for children.

Just as Washington's postwar years were touched with many intimations of mortality, so Martha had many somber occasions to reflect on life's brevity. In April 1785 an express messenger arrived at Mount Vernon bearing a double dose of dreadful news for her: her mother, seventy-five-year-old Frances Dandridge, and her last surviving brother, forty-eight-year-old Judge Bartholomew Dandridge, had died within nine days of each other. These deaths lengthened the already-long list of family losses Martha had endured, starting with the demise of her first husband and all four of her children. The death of her younger brother meant that, among her seven siblings, only her youngest sister, Betsy, was still alive. Like the Washingtons, the Dandridge clan seemed doomed to suffer untimely deaths.

The following year George Washington suffered two tremendous blows. He had always delighted in the bright young men in his military family, often finding it easier to befriend these protégés than his peers, and he had felt special warmth for Lieutenant Colonel Tench Tilghman, who handled his business matters in Baltimore. "I have often repeated to you that there are few men in the world to whom I am more sincerely attached by inclination than I am to you," Washington had assured him.[35] Genial and unassuming, Tilghman had entered fully into Washington's confidence, and the latter was grief-stricken when the younger man died at age forty-one in April 1786. In a mighty tribute, Washington told Jefferson that his former aide had "as fair a reputation as ever belonged to a human character," and he speculated that he mourned the death more keenly than anyone outside of Tilghman's own family.[36]

Perhaps more consequential for America's future was the demise of General Nathanael Greene at forty-three. Just as Washington and Greene had seen eye to eye on war-related matters, so they had viewed the country's postwar turmoil with similar apprehension. Like Washington, Greene had developed a federal perspective and feared that the total autonomy of the states would culminate in feuding and anarchy. As he warned Washington, "Many people secretly wish that every state should be completely independent and that, as soon as our public debts are liquidated, that Congress should be no more—a plan that would be as fatal to our interest at home as ruinous to it abroad."[37] Unfortunately, Greene's personal finances were in no less disorderly a state than those of the country at large: he had accumulated such heavy debts guaranteeing contracts for the southern army that it gave him "much pain and preyed heavily upon my spirits."[38] He also revealed to Washington in August 1784 that for two months he had experienced a "dangerous and disagree[able] pain" in his chest, which sounds like heart disease.[39] In June 1786, while at his estate near Savannah, Georgia, he was seized at the table with a "violent pain in his eye and head," followed by his death a few days later.[40]

Washington mourned Greene's death for many months. Beyond personal grief, he knew that the country had lost a man cut out for bigger things. He had counted on Greene as a political ally and kindred spirit and said he regretted "the death of this valuable character, especially at this crisis, when the political machine seems pregnant with the most awful events."[41] It seems likely that, had Greene lived, Washington would have chosen him as the first secretary of war in preference to Henry Knox. Greene died in such dire economic straits that Washington volunteered to pay for the education of his son, George Washington Greene. It was yet another example of Washington's extraordinary generosity in caring for the offspring of friends and family, whatever his own financial stringency.

CHAPTER FORTY-TWO

A Masterly Hand

FOR A MAN WHO EMPHASIZED HIS DISCOMFORT when posing for artists, George Washington dedicated an extraordinary amount of time to having his likeness preserved for posterity. As shown by his constant attention to his papers, he guarded his fame with vigilance. Sensitive to charges of self-promotion—charges that seemed to ring in his ears alone—he preferred sitting for artists when he could cite a plausible political excuse for doing so. Such was the case in the late summer of 1783, when Congress commissioned an equestrian statue of him and gave the prestigious assignment to artist Joseph Wright, who had the perfect pedigree to appease Washington's strict conscience. His mother, Patience Wright, a Quaker sculptor from Philadelphia, specialized in waxwork portraits. While mother and son were based in wartime London, she had patented a unique form of espionage by relaying secret messages to Benjamin Franklin and American politicians at home through messages sealed inside her waxed heads.

After studying with Benjamin West in London, Joseph Wright returned to America and received the coveted commission for the Washington statue. He began with an oil portrait of the general that many deemed "a better likeness of me than any other painter has done," Washington conceded.[1] Washington was then residing at Rocky Hill, outside Princeton, giving him time for this diversion. Protective of his image and afraid of appearing pretentious, Washington rebuffed Wright's request that he don a Roman toga. As a result, the painting is plain and powerfully realistic, showing a uniformed but unadorned Washington who eschews the standard props of power. Wright caught the weighty toll that the war years had exacted on Washington, whose face is long, gaunt, and devoid of animation; his eyes lack sparkle or luster. The nose is thick and straight and blunter than in earlier portraits. As Washington commented justly about Wright's style, "His forte seems to be in giving the distinguishing characteristics with more boldness than delicacy."[2] The painting also pinpointed an important quirk of Washington's face: the lazy right eye that slid off into the corner while the left eye stared straight ahead.

To prepare for the equestrian statue, Wright crafted a life mask of Washington's face with plaster of paris. Cooperating with artists brought out a certain drollery in Washington, and work on the mask led to a charming comic vignette with Martha Washington. As Washington recalled, the artist "oiled my features over, and, placing me flat upon my back upon a cot, proceeded to daub my face with the plaster. Whilst [I was] in this ludicrous attitude, Mrs. Washington entered the room, and, seeing my face thus overspread with the plaster, involuntarily exclaimed [in alarm]. Her cry excited in me a disposition to smile, which gave my mouth a slight twist . . . that is now observable in the bust which Wright afterward made."[3] Although Wright constructed the preparatory bust, he never completed the equestrian statue.

Another eminent artist with a special claim to Washington's time was Robert Edge Pine, who had lived near George William and Sally Fairfax in Bath, England. A vocal supporter of American independence, Pine had consulted the Fairfaxes about a controversial print Pine executed showing the "oppressions and calamities of America" and portraying Washington as the country's heroic liberator, as George William informed Washington.[4] It was a courageous action for an artist with a wife and six daughters and earned him "so many enemies in this selfish nation that he is compelled to go to America to seek bread in his profession."[5] There was no way Washington could reject an artist who kept alive the link with George William and Sally Fairfax.

On April 28, 1785, Pine arrived at Mount Vernon, intending to paint Washington for a grand sequence of works about the American Revolution. Earlier in his life, Washington said, he had been as restive "as a colt is of the saddle" when sitting for artists, but he was now amused at how docile he had become. "I am so hackneyed to the touches of the painter's pencil that I am now altogether at their beck and sit like Patience on a monument whilst they are delineating the lines of my face."[6] Pine spent three weeks at Mount Vernon and must have ingratiated himself with the entire family, for Washington agreed to additional portraits of Martha, all four of her grandchildren, and Fanny Bassett.

The most elaborate effort to capture Washington's image was the brilliant, painstaking work of an illustrious French sculptor. In June 1784 the Virginia legislature decided to commission a statue of Washington "of the finest marble and best workmanship" to grace the rotunda of the new state capitol in Richmond.[7]

Governor Harrison turned to Jefferson and Franklin in Paris to identify the "most masterly hand" for the job.[8] Assuming that a European sculptor would simply work from a painting, Harrison had Charles Willson Peale forward a full-length portrait of Washington. This simplistic conception of the job scarcely anticipated the complex demands of the formidable genius recruited by Jefferson and Franklin: Jean-Antoine Houdon, who was famous for his naturalistic style. The premier sculptor at European courts, he asked for a colossal fee, but Jefferson bargained him down to a thousand guineas.

Jefferson and Franklin artfully persuaded Washington to work with the French sculptor, Jefferson saying that Houdon was "the first statuary in the world" and had excitedly agreed to the assignment. In case Washington didn't comprehend the high honor involved, Jefferson mentioned that Houdon was currently finishing a statue of Louis XVI and had crafted a celebrated bust of Voltaire. Knowing that Houdon worked with fanatic intensity, Jefferson thought he should prepare Washington for the sculptor's exhausting demands. Houdon was, Jefferson wrote, "so enthusiastically fond of being the executor of this work that he offers to go himself to America for the purpose of forming your bust from the life, leaving all his business here in the meantime. He thinks that being three weeks with you would suffice to make his model of plaster, with which he will return here, and the work will employ him three years."[9] With two transatlantic crossings ahead of him and a projected absence from Paris of six months, Houdon insisted that Jefferson take out an insurance policy on his life for that time.

Cognizant of Washington's highly organized existence, Jefferson took a huge risk when he told Washington that, if Franklin concurred in selecting Houdon, "we shall send him over [at once], not having time to ask your permission and await your answer."[10] Fortunately, Houdon's sailing was delayed for several months due to illness. To ensure that Washington didn't back out, Jefferson informed him that Houdon had turned down an assignment from Catherine the Great of Russia to sculpt Washington, "which he considers as promising the brightest chapter of his history."[11] In a follow-up letter, Franklin said that, since the Europeans despaired of ever coaxing Washington across the ocean, they needed an excellent bust by Houdon to supply his place.

The only way that Washington could feel comfortable with such royal attention was to remind everyone that he was a purely passive recipient of the honor. Writing to Houdon, he stressed that, although the commission was "not of my seeking, I feel the most agreeable and grateful sensations."[12] On Sunday night, October 2, 1785, Houdon made a dramatic entrance at Mount Vernon, pulling up to the dock at eleven P.M. Washington was already in bed when the household was roused by the famous Frenchman, three young assistants, and an interpreter. In his diary, Washington pointedly noted that Houdon had come from nearby Alexandria, implying that he could easily have waited until morning instead of pouncing upon him at night. Anyone who knew Washington's rigid daily schedule and stern sense of decorum would have avoided this faux pas. A room was hastily prepared for these newcomers babbling in an exotic tongue.

The conscientious Houdon had brought along calipers and, when he got to work, proceeded to make meticulous measurements of Washington's body. He also asked if he could shadow Washington on his daily rounds and study his face and movements in social interactions. During the next two weeks he even attended a funeral with Washington and took part in the wedding of George Augustine Washington and Fanny Bassett. It reveals a good deal about Houdon's genius that the most expressive moment for him came when Washington flared up indignantly as he haggled over a pair of horses; always a tough bargainer, Washington thought the other trader was asking too much. During this sudden flash of anger, Houdon thought he spied the inner steel in Washington's nature.

Methodical in his own habits, Washington was naturally fascinated by the systematic effort that Houdon poured into each step of the artistic process. On October 6 the Frenchman began working on a terra-cotta bust that was likely a preliminary step in creating the full-length sculpture. The bust may have been dried in a Mount Vernon oven ordinarily reserved for baking. Houdon gave it as a gift to Washington, who treasured it in his private study for the rest of his life. Many people credited it as being the best likeness of him ever done. To the extent possible, Houdon dispensed with artistic conventions and pared down the bust to essential truths about Washington, making him life-size and lifelike. The sculpted face is strong and commanding, and the skin smooth, without the crags time later carved into the cheeks. As Washington turns his head, his shrewdly appraising eyes seem to scan the far horizon. Washington's expression is forceful, his determination evident in his narrow gaze, matched by the muscular strength of his shoulders. Because his hair isn't fluffed out at the sides, the bust accentuates the hard, lean strength of his face. Houdon captured both the aggressive and the cautious sides of Washington, held in perfect equipoise.

On October 10 Houdon moved on to preparing the plaster of paris for the life mask. Washington was so riveted by this procedure that he made an extended diary entry about it, describing how Houdon sifted the plaster until it obtained the consistency of thick cream, then mixed it with water and beat the combination with an iron spoon. The sculptor himself covered Washington's face with wet plaster in the few minutes before it began to harden and inserted a pair of quills in his nostrils for breathing. Nelly Custis never forgot her fright when she saw Washington laid out like a corpse in a morgue:

I was only six years old at the time and perhaps should not have retained any recollection of Houdon and his visit, had I not seen the General, as I supposed, dead and laid out on a table cover[e]d with a sheet. I was passing the white servants hall and saw, as I thought, the corpse of one I consider[e]d my father. I went in and found the general extended on his back on a large table, a sheet over him, except his face, on which Houdon was engaged in putting on plaster to form the cast. Quills were in the nostrils. I was very much alarmed until I was told that it was a bust, a likeness of the general, and would not injure him.[13]

The life mask repaid the effort applied to its preparation, and Houdon proudly called it "the most perfect reproduction of Washington's own face."[14] Showing Washington's face at rest, the mask's expression is gentle and pensive yet also powerful because of the strong cheekbones and musculature. Due to the loss of teeth on the left side, with the attendant bone decay, Washington's asymmetrical chin slants down obliquely to the right.

On October 17, as abruptly as they had appeared, Houdon and his assistants packed up their implements, marched down to the dock, and boarded Washington's barge for the short ride to Alexandria, where they caught a stagecoach bound for Philadelphia. Acknowledging Houdon's tremendous investment of time, Washington praised the French sculptor "for his trouble and risk of crossing the seas."[15] During the winter, Jefferson wrote to say that Houdon had arrived safely in Paris with the life mask, from which he would sculpt the standing statue for the Virginia capitol. Jefferson then posed an odd question: How would Washington like to be costumed in the sculpture? Once again Washington opted for modern dress in lieu of a Roman toga. The manner in which he expressed this to Jefferson betrayed his old provincial insecurity, as if he weren't sure he was entitled to an opinion in the artistic sphere and feared committing an error:

I have only to observe that not having a sufficient knowledge in the art of sculpture to oppose my judgment to the taste of connoisseurs, I do not desire to dictate in the matter. On the contrary, I shall be perfectly satisfied with whatever may be judged decent and proper. I should even scarcely have ventured to suggest that perhaps a servile adherence to the garb of antiquity might not be altogether so expedient as some little deviation in favor of the modern custom, if I had not learnt from Colo. Humphreys that this was a circumstance hinted in conversation by Mr [Benjamin] West to Houdon. This taste, which has been introduced in painting by West, I understand is received with applause and prevails extensively.[16]

Washington is quite knowing in his comment, although he advances it with a touching timidity.

No less a perfectionist than Washington, Houdon toiled for years over the Richmond statue, which wasn't set in the capitol rotunda until 1796. In the final version, Houdon played on the Cincinnatus theme of Washington returning to Mount Vernon and divesting himself of the instruments of war. Still dressed in uniform, his outer coat unbuttoned, Washington seems quietly self-possessed, his great labor finished. He has exchanged his sword for a walking stick in his right hand while his left arm rests on a column topped by his riding cape. He is tall and proud, erect and graceful, as he gazes into the bountiful future of his country. With true humility, Washington had asked to have the sculpture life-size instead of larger than life, and Houdon had heeded this noble request.

During that fall of 1785 Washington entertained another French visitor at Mount Vernon who was much less famous than Houdon but probably no less welcome. The dentist Jean-Pierre Le Mayeur had stayed in close touch with Washington ever since he visited the Continental Army's headquarters in 1783. During the summer of 1784 he spent enough time with the Washington family to become a close companion and endeared himself to Washy through the gift of a toy wooden horse. We know that Washington bought nine teeth that year from slaves for either implants or dentures in his own mouth. Wanting to stay in Le Mayeur's good graces, Washington promoted his career and furnished him with introductory letters to political luminaries in Virginia. Le Mayeur was such a frequent visitor at Mount Vernon, showing up three times in June 1786 alone, that he and Washington became fast friends. The dentist was a fancier of horseflesh, and Washington allowed him to drop off his mares to be serviced by his famous stallion Magnolio. For all the ingenuity Le Mayeur devoted to Washington's teeth, he couldn't seem to arrest the decay, and Washington continued to lose teeth. Martha Washington had previously had a cheerier history with her teeth, but by now she too had been fitted out with dentures in what must have become a new form of marital compatibility.

Even as Houdon worked on his statue of Washington, which reflected a hopeful stance toward America's future, the latter was heartsick at the country's disarray and feared that peace would undo the valiant work accomplished by the Continental Army. His complaints about the Articles of Confederation were consistent with those voiced during the war. The government had no real executive branch, just an endless multiplicity of committees. The few executive departments were adjuncts of a chaotic, ramshackle Congress, which Washington condemned as "wretchedly managed."[17] This legislative body required a quorum of nine states to do business; operated on a one-state, one-vote basis; and could pass major laws only with a unanimous vote. The United States wasn't a country but a confederation of thirteen autonomous states, loosely presided over by Congress. The states' blatant selfishness frustrated any effort to run a sound national government, which had no real enforcement powers over them. As Washington phrased it in a letter, "We are either a united people under one head . . . or we are thirteen independent sovereignties, eternally counteracting each other."[18] Americans now defined themselves as the antithesis of everything English, even if that acted to their detriment.

Thanks to congressional impotence, the government was unable to repay creditors who had financed the Revolution. The paper issued to them now traded at a tiny fraction of its face value, and Congress was powerless to redeem it. Still lacking an independent revenue source, Congress could request money from the states but not compel them to pay. Meanwhile America was fast becoming an irredeemably profligate nation. Despite his own checkered history with London creditors, Washington was adamant that Americans should pay their prewar debts to England, as stipulated in the peace treaty. The federal government also lacked the power to regulate trade among states or with foreign nations. Many states imposed duties on goods from neighboring states, and as Madison cynically interpreted it for Jefferson, "the predominant seaport states were fleecing their neighbors."[19] The resulting trade disputes led to scorching interstate battles. As England imposed restrictions on American trade in the West Indies, the federal government was helpless to retaliate. Without such power, Washington thought, the United States could never negotiate commercial treaties or bargain advantageously with other countries. If the states tried individually to regulate trade, he warned, "an abortion or a many-headed monster would be the issue."[20]

Washington also perceived a pressing need for American military power. Still hemmed in by hostile foreign nations in North America, the country had a federal army of fewer than a thousand men. England refused to surrender a string of forts that stretched in a broad arc from the St. Lawrence River to the Great Lakes and the Ohio Valley. Spain also figured as a threat. The peace treaty had granted the United States the territory between the Appalachian Mountains and the Mississippi. This produced friction with Spain, which shut the lower Mississippi River to American commerce, threatening the livelihood of restive western farmers. There was a more distant threat to peace: in 1785 Barbary pirates from northern Africa began preying on American merchant vessels, which no longer enjoyed the protection of the British Navy. "Would to Heaven we had a navy to reform those enemies to mankind or crush them into non-existence," Washington told Lafayette.[21] There was no way to create a sizable army or navy without shoring up federal power.

Perhaps most disturbing to Washington was the prospect that liberty would descend into anarchy. Some populist demagogue, he feared, might exploit the weakness of a feeble central government to establish a dictatorship. Where Jefferson and Madison dreaded a powerful national government as the primrose path to monarchy, Washington and Hamilton continued to view a strong central government as the best bulwark against that threat. "What astonishing changes a few years are capable of producing!" Washington exclaimed to John Jay in 1786. "I am told that even respectable characters speak of a monarchical form of government without horror."[22]

George Washington trusted the long-term wisdom of the American people, but his deep, abiding faith was often qualified in the short run by a pessimistic view. In 1786 he expressed this ambivalence to Madison: "No morn ever dawned more favorable than ours did—and no day was ever more clouded than the present!"[23] Washington was amazingly sensitive to America's unseen audience of European skeptics. Far from thumbing his nose at such doomsday prophets, he wanted to prove them wrong and earn their good opinion. In advocating enlarged powers for Congress, he said that it was "evident to me we never shall establish a national character, or be considered on a respectable footing by the powers of Europe," unless this was accomplished.[24] That Washington responded so keenly to European derision reveals, once again, residual traces of his old insularity. On some level he remained the country cousin, eager to vindicate his country's worth in the metropolitan hubs of Europe.

As someone who thought people should look to the educated, well-to-do members of the community for leadership, Washington had an instinctive sense of public service. From the time he returned to Mount Vernon after the war, his mind dwelled actively on political problems. He must have sensed he would be allowed only a brief interval of repose before being plunged back into the hurly-burly of politics. As political power reverted back to state capitals, he might have guessed that the nucleus of any future federal government would come from the general staff of the Continental Army, which had experienced so dramatically the perils of an ineffective government. His comforting fantasy of a serene Mount Vernon retirement began to fade. "Retired as I am from the world," he told Jay during the summer of 1786, "I frankly acknowledge I cannot feel myself an unconcerned spectator." Then he backed away from the implications of that statement: "Yet having happily assisted in bringing the ship into port and having been fairly discharged, it is not my business to embark again on a sea of troubles."[25]

At times Washington pretended that he was too remote from political affairs to know what Americans thought about key issues, telling Jefferson, "Indeed, I am too much secluded from the world to know with certainty what sensation the refusal of the British to deliver up the western posts has made on the public mind."[26] Such protestations of ignorance flew in the face of several factors: Washington entertained a large, heterogeneous group of visitors at Mount Vernon; he subscribed to many gazettes; and he conducted a rich correspondence with political intimates. As early as March 1786 he heard from Jay about a movement gathering force to revise the Articles of Confederation. While sympathetic, Washington told him that implementing those changes would require a crisis atmosphere: "That it is necessary to revise and amend the Articles of Confederation, I entertain *no* doubt. But what may be the consequences of such an attempt is doubtful. Yet, something must be done or the fabric must fall."[27] By that summer Washington sounded as if things had reached a critical impasse, and he described the country's state as "shameful and disgusting."[28] In mid-August he believed that a great turning point was at hand. "Your sentiments, that our affairs are drawing rapidly to a crisis, accord with my own," he assured Jay.[29]

One man shaping Washington's views was James Madison. On a Saturday evening in early September 1785, Madison had appeared at Mount Vernon and was quickly closeted in conversation with Washington, lingering through breakfast on Monday morning. A rigorous political theorist with a coolly skeptical intellect, the diminutive, bookish Madison was alarmed by the irresponsible behavior of the state legislatures. Though just thirty-four, he seemed prematurely aged, with thinning hair combed flat atop his head. His dark, intense eyes stared from a pale face with heavy eyebrows. Only five foot four and plagued by delicate health, he was abstemious in his habits. To some, he seemed an austere personality. The wife of one Virginia politician called him "a gloomy stiff creature," while another woman found him "mute, cold, and repulsive."[30] He was wont to croak and mumble, could scarcely be heard during speeches, and was painfully retiring at first meeting. Nevertheless, with his political allies and students of history, Madison could be an absorbing conversationalist. "He is peculiarly interesting in conversation, cheerful, gay, and full of anecdote . . . sprightly, varied, fertile in his topics, and felicitous in his descriptions and illustrations," wrote Jared Sparks, an early editor of Washington's papers.[31]

Appearances could be deceiving with James Madison. However professorial in manner, he was the largest slaveholder in Orange County, Virginia, and his fragile health masked a fanatic determination. Never a pushover in political debates, he plumbed every subject to the bottom and was invariably the best-prepared person in the room. To prepare for the revision of the Articles of Confederation, he plowed through an entire "literary cargo" of books that Jefferson forwarded from Paris.[32] For a young man, he possessed extensive legislative experience, first as an effective member of Congress and now as a member of the Virginia assembly. A skillful legislator, secretive and canny, he exerted his influence in mysteriously indirect ways. Political foes who underrated James Madison did so at their peril.

In September 1786, Madison attended a conference in Annapolis ostensibly devoted to interstate commerce. Here commissioners from five states discussed ways to resolve the trade disputes roiling the country. The Annapolis conference determined that the only way to cure trade disputes was to perform radical surgery on the Articles of Confederation. One of the commissioners, Alexander Hamilton, drafted a bold communiqué calling upon the thirteen states to send delegates to a convention in Philadelphia in May 1787 that would "render the constitution of the federal government adequate to the exigencies of the union."[33] Two days after the Annapolis meeting, Edmund Randolph, head of the Virginia delegation, arrived at Mount Vernon to brief Washington, who fully endorsed Hamilton's appeal. In late October Madison, accompanied by James Monroe, spent another three days at Mount Vernon and found common ground with Washington as they dissected the Articles of Confederation. Clearly Madison, Monroe, and Randolph were trying to cajole Washington from retirement and enlist him in the growing movement to reform the political structure. He was slowly being swept up in a swelling tide that he would find difficult to resist.

As Washington considered his future role, an outbreak of violence in rural Massachusetts sharpened the reform debate. If ever American history had a useful crisis, it occurred in western Massachusetts in the autumn of 1786. To retire a heavy debt load, the state had boosted land taxes and thereby provoked the wrath of farmers, many of whom lost their land in foreclosures. Led by Daniel Shays, a militia captain during the war, thousands of rebels, heaving pitchforks, swarmed into rural courthouses to menace judges and block foreclosures. Invoking the Revolution's militant spirit, many donned old uniforms from the Continental Army. When they threatened to march on the army arsenal in Springfield, Congress rushed Henry Knox to the scene to supervise defensive measures. Henry Lee sent Washington an alarming report about the rebels' plans to subvert state government, abolish debt, and redistribute property: "In one word, my dear General, we are all in dire apprehension that a beginning of anarchy, with all its calamities, has approached." Citizens appealed to Washington to go to Massachusetts, saying his steadying presence would "bring them back to peace and reconciliation."[34]

The events in Massachusetts struck the law-abiding Washington with horror, and the pitch of his letters instantly rose in intensity. "But for God's sake, tell me, what is the cause of all these commotions?" he asked David Humphreys. If there were legitimate grievances, why had they not been redressed? If it was merely a case of licentiousness, why didn't the government step in at once? "Commotions of this sort, like snowballs, gather strength as they roll, if there is no opposition in the way to divide and crumble them."[35] Once again Washington feared disgrace among Europeans, who would seize upon any lapse to validate their cynical view of America, and this became a leitmotif of his letters during the Massachusetts crisis: "I am really mortified beyond expression that, in the moment of our acknowledged independence, we should by our conduct verify the predictions of our transatlantic foe and render ourselves ridiculous and contemptible in the eyes of all Europe."[36] However much he wished to refute these skeptics, Washington had clearly internalized their doubts.

In late October Knox told Washington that the rebels paid little in taxes and had seized on that issue as a pretext to wage class warfare. He warned of the insidious spread of a radical leveling doctrine. "They feel at once their own poverty, compared with the opulent," he said, and want to convert private property into "the common property of all."[37] Overstating the menace, Knox conjured up a desperate army of twelve thousand to fifteen thousand young men prowling New England and challenging lawful government. If this movement spread, he thought, the country would be drawn into the horror of civil war. From New Haven, David Humphreys predicted that a civil war would flush Washington from retirement, forcing him to take sides: "In case of civil discord, I have already told you, it was seriously my opinion that you could not remain neuter and that you would be obliged, in self defence, to take part on one side or the other."[38]

For Washington, who cherished his retirement, this news must have been disturbing. Not surprisingly, Shays's Rebellion crystallized for him the need to overhaul the Articles of Confederation. "What stronger evidence can be given of the want of energy in our governments than these disorders?" he asked Madison. "If there exists not a power to check them, what security has a man of life, liberty, or property?"[39] What most troubled Washington was that people were flouting a political order for which they had recently risked their lives: "It is but the other day we were shedding our blood to obtain the constitutions under which we now live—constitutions of our own choice and framing—and now we are unsheathing the sword to overturn them!"[40]

The Massachusetts uprising terminated in a full-blown military confrontation. In late January Shays and his followers marched on the Springfield arsenal, intending to seize its stores of muskets and powder, when a Massachusetts militia fired point-blank into the crowd, killing several rebels. The next day General Benjamin Lincoln arrived with four thousand soldiers and dispersed the remnants of the dissident army, ending the protest. Even though Washington had supported the overwhelming show of force, once the insurrection was broken, he favored leniency for the culprits, showing how subtly he could parse the political demands of a complex situation. That Congress had abdicated its role in squashing the protest again exposed a dangerous vacuum of national power. Madison believed that Shays's Rebellion "contributed more to that uneasiness which produced the constitution and prepared the public mind for a general reform" than all the defects of the Articles of Confederation combined.[41] It made it almost certain that George Washington's days as a Virginia planter were numbered.

CHAPTER FORTY-THREE

A House on Fire

IN LATE 1786 George Washington's life was again thrown into turmoil when Madison informed him that the Virginia legislature planned to name him head of the state's seven-man delegation at the forthcoming convention in Philadelphia. Having made no effort to join the group, Washington was cast into a terrible state of indecision. "Never was my embarrassment or hesitation more extreme or distressing," he wrote.[1] Deep questioning was typical of Washington's political style. Holding himself aloof, he had learned to set a high price on his participation, yielding only with reluctance. Whenever his reputation was at stake, he studied every side of a decision, analyzing how his actions would be perceived. Having learned to accumulate power by withholding his assent, he understood the influence of his mystique and kept people in suspense.

Complicating his attendance in Philadelphia was that he had already declined to attend the triennial meeting of the Society of the Cincinnati, which by an extraordinary coincidence was also slated for May 1787 in Philadelphia. He had just sent out a mailing to members, explaining that he would neither attend nor stand for reelection as president. It irked him that many state chapters had voted down his proposed reforms, especially the one banning the hereditary provision. He had wanted to remain with the organization long enough to dispel any speculation that he had repudiated its principles. Now that the dissent had died down, he thought it an opportune moment to extricate himself. In declining the invitation, he also cited the press of private business and "the present imbecility of my health, occasioned by a violent attack of the fever and ague, succeeded by rheumatic pains (to which till of late I have been an entire stranger)."[2]

If Washington used his health problems as an excuse, he didn't conjure them from thin air. In late August 1786 he had contracted a "fever and ague" that lasted for two weeks. Since Dr. Craik prescribed the bark of the cinchona tree, a natural source of quinine, one suspects a recurrence of the malaria that had pestered him as a young soldier. Despite early illnesses, the younger Washington had been mostly a picture of ruddy health. Now as aches and pains invaded his body, he was losing his youthful grace, and he complained to Madison of feeling his rheumatic pains "very sensibly."[3] These pains became so debilitating that he couldn't "raise my hand to my head or turn myself in bed."[4] By April 1787, to counter this sharp pain, he had to immobilize his arm in a sling. He went from having a boundless sense of health to feeling his age abruptly—what he called "descending the hill"—and may have wondered whether he possessed the necessary fund of energy for the momentous political challenges ahead.[5] Washington may also have worried anew about his poor genetic endowment after his favorite brother, John Augustine, yet another short-lived Washington male, died suddenly in early January from what Washington called "a fit of gout in the head."[6]

On November 18 Washington explained to Madison that, having spurned the Cincinnati meeting, he couldn't attend the Constitutional Convention without being caught in an embarrassing lie, "giving offense to a very respectable and deserving part of the community—the late officers of the American Army."[7] Were it not for this dilemma, he said, he would certainly attend an event so vital to the national welfare. He wanted to be true to the principles of the Revolution, but he also wanted to be faithful to his colleagues, a sacred trust for him. In his 1783 circular letter to the states, he had solemnly pledged that he would not reenter politics, a public vow that the honorable Washington took seriously. The mythology that he could not tell a lie had some basis in fact. He may also have hesitated to attend the Constitutional Convention from a premonition that it would initiate a sequence of events that would pull him away indefinitely from Mount Vernon. After all, the last time he heeded his country's call in a crisis, it had embroiled him in more than eight years of war.

Refusing to let Washington off the hook, Madison argued that his presence in Philadelphia would enhance the convention's credibility and attract "select characters" from every state.[8] In reply, Washington laid out his deeply conflicted feelings about the Cincinnati. He reviewed the organization's history, telling how it had started as a charitable fund for widows and saying that he never dreamed it would give birth to "jealousies" and "dangers" that threatened republican principles.[9] Washington stood in an acute bind: he didn't wish to insult his fellow officers, but he also refused to support measures he deemed incompatible with republican principles. His response to the predicament shows how delicately he could weigh conflicting claims and cloak the real reason behind an apparent one.

Writing to Governor Edmund Randolph on December 21, Washington formally declined appointment to the convention, secretly hoping his Virginia associates would drop the matter. But when Madison learned of Washington's decision, he requested that he keep the door ajar "in case the gathering clouds should become so dark and menacing as to supersede every consideration but that of our national existence or safety."[10] All winter long, Washington rested in a curious limbo vis-à-vis the convention. "My name is in the delegation to this convention," he told Jay, "but it was put there contrary to my desire and remains there contrary to my request."[11]

Washington was frankly baffled and, in his time-honored executive style, canvassed friends about how to resolve his dilemma, enlisting Madison, Humphreys, Knox, and Jay. Each exchange disclosed another layer of doubt on his part. To Humphreys, Washington confessed his fear that the Constitutional Convention might fail, much as he had been haunted by fear of failure when named commander in chief in 1775. Failure "would be a disagreeable predicament for any of them [the delegates] to be in, but more particularly so for a person in my situation," he wrote.[12] Since he personified the country, he stood to lose the most from accusations of partisanship. On the other hand, this might be a last opportunity to salvage a deteriorating nation. Any failure, he said, could be construed "as an unequivocal proof that the states are not likely to agree in any general measure . . . and consequently that there is an end put to federal government."[13] In soliciting opinions, he again preferred to give a passive appearance to active decisions, making it seem that he was being reluctantly borne along by fate, friends, or historical necessity, when he was actually shaping as well as reacting to events. This technique allowed him to cast himself into the modest role of someone answering the summons of history. It also permitted him to wait until a consensus had emerged on his course of action. If Washington could never entirely resist the allure of fame, neither could he openly welcome it.

Not all of Washington's advisers thought he should attend. Humphreys reminded him of the potentially illegal nature of the gathering and, consequently, the huge reputational risk. "I concur fully in sentiment with you concerning the inexpediency of your attending the convention," he wrote.[14] Knox favored Washington's going but felt obliged to point out that the Philadelphia convention might be "an irregular assembly," even an illegal one, since it would operate outside the amendment process spelled out in the Articles of Confederation. It might even expose delegates to conspiracy charges. On the other hand, Washington's presence would draw New England states that had boycotted the Annapolis conference, converting it into a truly national gathering. To pique Washington's interest, Jay sent him a clairvoyant sketch of a new government divided into legislative, executive, and judicial branches. "Let Congress legislate," he told Washington. "Let others execute. Let others judge."[15] The letter foreshadowed the exact shape of the future government.

During February and March 1787 Washington alternated between passionate concern for saving the union and an insistence that he couldn't go to Philadelphia. He likened the confederacy to a "house on fire," saying that unless emergency measures were taken, the building would be "reduced to ashes"; but somebody else would apparently have to extinguish the blaze.[16] Washington's internal deliberations began to shift on February 21, when Congress approved a convention "for the sole and express purpose of revising the Articles of Confederation."[17] While the convention ended up exceeding this mandate, the decision momentarily retired the legality issue. With the country "approaching to some awful crisis," he told Knox, he began to fret about a public outcry if he *didn't* go to Philadelphia.[18] Suddenly he seemed to lean in the other direction. "A thought, however, has lately run through my mind, which is attended with embarrassment," he confided to Knox in early March. "It is, whether my non-attendance in this convention will not be considered as a dereliction to republicanism."[19]

Wisely, Washington had allowed the issue to percolate for months, encouraging the perception that he was following rather than leading events. On March 19 Knox sent him a letter that may have clinched his decision. He said that he took it for granted that Washington would be elected president of the convention. If the convention still faltered and produced only a "patchwork to the present defective confederation, your reputation would in a degree suffer." But if the convention forged a vigorous new federal government, "it would be a circumstance highly honorable to your fame . . . and doubly entitle you to the glorious republican epithet 'The Father of Your Country.'"[20] This was the perfect double-barreled appeal to Washington's vanity and patriotism. Because of the high caliber of the delegates selected, Knox wagered that the convention would spawn a superior new system, and "therefore the balance of my opinion preponderates greatly in favor of your attendance."[21]

In retrospect, it seems foreordained that Washington, with his unerring sense of duty, would go to Philadelphia. He was a casualty of his own greatness, which dictated a path in life from which he couldn't deviate. Had he turned down the call to duty, he would have felt something incomplete in his grand mission to found the country, but he patently had to convince himself and the world of his purely disinterested motives. Now he could proceed as if summoned from self-imposed retirement by popular acclaim.

On March 28 Washington wrote to Governor Randolph and submitted to his fate: he would indeed attend the convention. He made it clear that he was doing so involuntarily and only submitting to the entreaties of friends. In Washington's life, however, one commitment led ineluctably to the next, and he acknowledged that his attendance would have "a tendency to sweep me back into the tide of public affairs."[22] To solve his dilemma with the Cincinnati, he planned to go to Philadelphia a week early and address the group, so they would not attribute his attending the Constitutional Convention instead "to a disrespectful inattention to the Society."[23] Henry Knox was bowled over by Washington's decision. "Secure as he was in his fame," he wrote to Lafayette, "he has again committed it to the mercy of events. Nothing but the critical situation of his country would have induced him to so hazardous a conduct."[24] Having made his decision, Washington gave unstinting support to a convention that would do far more than just tinker with the Articles of Confederation: like Madison, he wanted root-and-branch reform. He told Knox that the convention should "probe the defects" of the Articles of Confederation "to the bottom," and he worried that some states might not send delegates or would hobble them with "cramped powers," fostering an impasse.[25] By this point, Washington was clearly primed for decisive action in Philadelphia.

Before taking on the burden of America, Washington had to deal with a piece of unfinished family business: the chronic discontent of his mother. Mary Washington, with her flinty independence, was still stewing with grievances. Right before John Augustine died in early January, she had written to him to complain of an absence of corn at her four-hundred-acre farm in the Little Falls quarter of the Rappahannock River. "I never lived soe pore in my life," she insisted.[26] Had it not been for succor from a neighbor and her daughter, Betty, she contended, "I should be almost starvd, butt I am like an old almanack, quit out of date."[27] After Mary's wartime petition to the Virginia legislature, John Augustine, at George's behest, had taken charge of her mismanaged property. This letter about her supposed poverty shows that she did not restrict her whining to her famous son. She had mixed feelings about allowing others to govern her business. When her late son-in-law, Fielding Lewis, volunteered to take over her business affairs, Mary Washington had shot back, "Do you, Fielding, keep my books in order, for your eyesight is better than mine, but leave the executive management to me."[28]

News that Mary was again denigrating him drifted back to George, who wrote to her in mid-February and enclosed another fifteen guineas. In this stilted letter, Washington revealed that his relations with her had grown so frosty that the two hadn't even communicated after Jack's death. Indignant at his mother's accusation that he was being stingy, he poured out his grievances, explaining in brutal detail the miserable state of his finances:

> I have now demands upon me for more than 500£, three hundred and forty odd which is due for the tax of 1786; and I know not where, or when, I shall receive one shilling with which to pay. In the last two years, I made no crops. In the first I was

obliged to buy corn and this year have none to sell and my wheat is so bad that I cannot neither eat it myself nor sell it to others, and tobacco I make none. Those who owe me money cannot or will not pay it without [law]suits . . . whilst my expenses . . . for the absolute support of my family and the visitors who are constantly here are exceedingly high; higher indeed than I can support, without selling part of my estate, which I am disposed to do rather than run in debt . . . This is really and truly my situation.[29]

Washington went on to protest that, despite their business agreement, he had received not a penny from his mother's farm, even though he had paid 122 pounds in annual rent for her plantation and slaves; either Mary or her overseer had skimmed off the profits and forwarded nothing to him. Beyond that, he had given her more than 300 pounds in unpaid loans over a dozen years—all carefully documented in his ledgers. As a result of her accusations, he told her, "I am viewed as a delinquent and considered perhaps by the world as [an] unjust and undutiful son."[30] Once again Washington was preoccupied with a world that might sit in disapproving judgment upon him. To relieve his mother's distress, he suggested that she hire out her servants and live with one of her children. In fact, shortly before his death, John Augustine had volunteered to take her in.

Anticipating her next request, Washington said that she was welcome to live at Mount Vernon, but he warned her that "in truth it may be compared to a well-resorted tavern, as scarcely any strangers who are going from north to south, or from south to north, do not spend a day or two at it. This would, were you to be an inhabitant of it, oblige you to do one of 3 things, 1st to be always dressing to appear in company, 2d to come into [it] in a dishabille or 3d to be, as it were, a prisoner in your own chamber."[31] This image of Mount Vernon as a crowded, noisy inn, swarming with strangers, was not exactly an inviting one, and Mary never came to live there. The letter is conspicuously devoid of warmth or family affection: Washington and his mother were simply locked in an unhappy business relationship. Washington's reasons for dissuading his mother from living at Mount Vernon confirm that he perceived her as a coarse countrywoman who would be ill at ease in more polished society.

On March 7 Washington returned to Fredericksburg for what he imagined would be the "last act of personal duty"—that is, the last time he might see his aged mother.[32] Then in late April, as he prepared to leave for Philadelphia, he was summoned to Fredericksburg by news that both Mary, who was apparently suffering from breast cancer, and his sister, Betty, were gravely ill. Even though his arm now rested in a sling from rheumatic pain, Washington made the urgent trip to Fredericksburg, telling Henry Knox that he was "hastening to obey this melancholy call, after having just bid an eternal farewell to a much loved brother."[33] In correspondence, Washington always sounded like the conscientious son, telling Robert Morris that he had been called to Fredericksburg for "the last adieu to an honored parent and an affectionate sister."[34]

Although the trip proved a false alarm, Washington found his mother vastly changed, her illness having "reduced her to a skeleton, tho[ugh] she is somewhat amended."[35] Oddly, Washington had made no previous reference to her medical situation, which made her complaining far more comprehensible. Betty had improved as well and was now out of danger. One Fredericksburg resident was shocked by the transformation in Washington's own appearance: "Gen[era]l Washington has been here to see his mother, who has been ill . . . The Gen[era]l is much altered in his person, one arm swung with rheumatism."[36] After a few days Washington returned to Mount Vernon, but the trip must have formed a sobering backdrop to his journey to the Constitutional Convention.

On May 9, 1787, shortly after sunrise, George Washington set off for Philadelphia. While his rheumatic misery had abated, he was beset by other complaints, including a violent headache and an upset stomach—perhaps the somatic expression of his dread about the convention. Until this time Martha Washington had been the loyal, submissive wife in dealing with her husband's career. Now, as she saw George sentenced to life imprisonment in American politics, she began to rebel and decided to skip the Constitutional Convention. "Mrs. Washington is become too domestic, and too attentive to two little grandchildren to leave home," Washington explained to Robert Morris, "and I can assure you, sir, that it was not until after a long struggle [that] I could obtain my own consent to appear again in a public theater."[37] This was a more independent Martha than the one who had rushed off to her husband's winter camps despite her fears of travel and gunfire.

On Sunday, May 13, Washington arrived at Chester, Pennsylvania, and was escorted into Philadelphia by a long procession of dignitaries and a troop of light horse. Greeted by booming artillery and saluting officers, Washington must have been reminded of the worshipful attention he had generated during the war. Despite inclement weather, the sidewalks were densely packed with enthusiastic throngs. Noted the *Pennsylvania Packet,* "The joy of the people on the coming of this great and good man was shown by their acclamation and the ringing of bells."[38] Washington having shed his arm sling, the newspaper expressed joy in finding "our old and faithful commander in the full enjoyment of his health and fame."[39] Washington saw nothing incongruous about arriving in Philadelphia flanked by three of his slaves, Giles, Paris, and the durable Billy Lee; the fate of such slaves would form a contentious issue at the convention. Although James Madison hoped that the entire Virginia delegation would stay at the same lodging house, hard by the Pennsylvania

State House, Washington succumbed to the entreaties of Robert Morris and stayed with him and his wife, Mary.

Guided by a fine sense of decorum, Washington made his first courtesy call on the venerable Benjamin Franklin, whom he had not seen since 1776, and his elderly host broke open a cask of dark beer to receive him. Washington had long revered Franklin as a "wise, a great and virtuous man."[40] Throughout the war he had addressed the older man with exquisite respect, extending to him the title "Your Excellency" that the rest of the world also applied to him. After the war Franklin had tried to woo Washington into a joint tour of Europe, which would have made a sensation by uniting the two most famous Americans. Now, as president of the Executive Council of Pennsylvania, Franklin was Washington's only serious rival for the convention presidency. His medical situation, however, militated against his selection: he was tormented by gout and kidney stones, even though he tossed off witticisms about the latter. "You may judge that my disease is not grievous," he said, "since I am more afraid of the medicines than of the malady."[41]

The assembly of demigods got off to a rather sluggish start. Although the convention was supposed to begin on May 14, only the Virginia and Pennsylvania delegations arrived on time, forcing a delay. A punctual man, Washington was irritated by the absence of a quorum of seven states and groused to George Augustine that the deferrals were "highly vexatious to those who are idly and expensively spending their time here."[42] Throughout his time in Philadelphia, Washington plied George Augustine with detailed advice about Mount Vernon, just as he had with Lund Washington during the war. Two days after the convention opened, he asked his nephew if he had "tried both fresh and salt fish as a manure" and recommended that he plant buckwheat.[43] As a farmer, it frustrated him that Philadelphia was being drenched with rain while drought prevailed in Virginia.

The delay thrust Washington into a knotty predicament vis-à-vis the Society of the Cincinnati, for it suddenly gave him time to attend their meetings. Reluctant to become more deeply involved, he came up with a clever alternative. Instead of attending meetings, he dined on May 15 with twenty members of the society, thus preserving a self-protective distance. Because he didn't wish to affront old comrades, he accepted reelection as president on May 18, making clear that the actual duties would devolve on the vice president. That he steered clear of the Cincinnati was fine with the more diehard members, one saying, "I could almost wish for the absence of the illustrious chief, whose extreme prudence and circumspection . . . may cool our laudable and necessary ebullition with a few drops, if not a torrent, of cold water."[44]

While awaiting the convention's start, Washington hobnobbed with tony members of Philadelphia society, starting with Robert and Mary White Morris. Among his other hosts were the wealthy William Bingham and his beautiful wife, Anne Willing Bingham, whose splendid house on Third Street formed the centerpiece of Philadelphia society. There was nothing surprising in Washington's seeking out such rich company: their social milieu was the same as his at home. Very receptive, as always, to the ladies, he noted in his diary any feminine company he shared. He attended a charity event with Mary White Morris "and some other ladies" to hear a Mrs. O'Connell deliver a discourse on eloquence.[45] Later in the week he attended a wedding for the daughter of Benjamin Chew, whose stone house in Germantown had presented such a costly obstacle to the Continental Army. He evidently enjoyed it: "Drank tea there in a very large circle of ladies."[46] One wonders whether Washington enjoyed this brief vacation from Martha's company.

Washington renewed an important friendship, formed during the First Continental Congress, with the wealthy, laconic Samuel Powel, a former mayor of Philadelphia, and his sophisticated, entrancing wife, Elizabeth (or Eliza). The Powels inhabited a three-story rococo mansion on Third Street that was so tastefully opulent that the Chevalier de Chastellux had praised this "handsome house . . . adorned with fine prints and some very good copies of the best Italian paintings."[47] But during the First Continental Congress, the puritanical John Adams had recoiled from the "sinful feast" he attended there, which had everything that "could delight the eye or allure the taste."[48] George Washington had no such trouble with the regal atmosphere at the Powels' and was a frequent guest at their soirées.

An immensely charming, erudite, and witty woman, who wrote with literary flair and elegance, Elizabeth Willing Powel eclipsed her stolid husband and could have held her own in the spirited repartee of any European salon. The daughter as well as the wife of a mayor, this socially proficient and politically opinionated hostess loved to flirt with powerful men, and George Washington fell under her spell. A portrait by Matthew Pratt shows an extremely handsome older woman whose low-cut yellow dress and purple sash amply display her voluptuous figure. She looks calm and poised, with a penetrating eye and a slightly melancholy air after the death of her two sons. Elizabeth Powel provided virtually the only instance in his later years when Washington befriended a couple but was much closer with the wife. She revered Washington, whom she saw on a par with the loftiest heroes of antiquity. As with George William and Sally Fairfax, Washington was careful to stay on good terms with Samuel Powel and equally careful to include Martha Washington in the friendship. Nevertheless, his friendship with Elizabeth Powel was his only deep, direct one with a woman who qualified as an intellectual peer and treated him as such. In this relationship Washington escaped the narrow bounds of marriage, met Powel alone for teas, and corresponded with her. We have no evidence that their closeness ever progressed beyond that, but if George Washington ever contemplated romance with another woman, it surely must have been Elizabeth Powel.

One of Samuel Powel's hobbies was making silhouettes, and he got Washington to sit for one. It was a measure of Washington's regard for his image that he faulted the silhouette for a small wattle sagging from his chin and asked Powel to redo the portrait. The drooping chin was duly excised from the finished product.

For all his mixing in high society, Washington was an extremely hardworking delegate at the convention. At some point before it started, he took the ideas for constitutional reform presented to him by Jay, Knox, and Madison and boiled them down into a handy digest. Back in 1776 he had delivered a comment on Virginia's new constitution that shows how studiously he approached such work: "To form a new government requires infinite care and unbounded attention, for if the foundation is badly laid, the superstructure must be bad."[49]

Because the entire Virginia delegation arrived on time, its members developed a powerful early cohesion. Headed by Governor Edmund Randolph, the distinguished group included Madison and George Mason; the latter informed his son that the hardworking Virginians met "two or three hours every day in order to form a proper correspondence of sentiments."[50] Their deliberations yielded the so-called Virginia Plan, spearheaded by Madison, which proposed for a tripartite government and proportional representation in both houses of Congress. Madison and Washington, who favored a vigorous central government, carried the day against objections from Randolph and Mason, making their strongly nationalist views the official opening position of the Virginia delegation.

On a rainy Friday, May 25, the convention obtained its seven-state quorum and began to meet officially. It had been decided that Franklin would nominate Washington as president. When the ailing Franklin was grounded by heavy rain, he asked Robert Morris to nominate Washington in his stead. (When Franklin finally did arrive at the sessions, he had to be carried aloft in a sedan chair, hoisted by four convicts from the Walnut Street jail.) The delegates appreciated Franklin's magnanimous gesture, and Madison wrote that "the nomination came with particular grace from Pennsylvania, as Dr. Franklin alone could have been thought of as a competitor."[51] After being seconded by John Rutledge, Washington was unanimously elected the convention president, while Major William Jackson, who had been on General Lincoln's wartime staff, became its secretary.

After Washington was chosen, Morris and Rutledge accompanied him to a tall wooden chair in front, placed on an elevated platform and adorned with a rising sun on its carved back. Perhaps to conjure up the spirit of 1776 or remind delegates of his military garb at the Second Continental Congress, Washington appeared in his old uniform. He made a short acceptance speech, full of vintage touches, including confessions of inadequacy and a plea for understanding if he failed—pretty much the same speech he made after every major appointment in his life. As recorded by Madison, Washington "reminded them of the novelty of the scene of business in which he was to act, lamented his want of [better qualifications], and claimed the indulgence of the house towards the involuntary errors which his inexperience might occasion."[52]

The post of president raised Washington to a nonpartisan, nonspeaking role—ideal for his discreet nature. The Constitutional Convention was yet another situation where the need for national unity imposed a congenial silence upon him. It spared him the need to voice opinions or make speeches, enabling him to bridge divisions and restricting his lobbying to the social hours. He followed the debates closely and later said he "attentively heard and read every oral and printed information on both sides of the question that could be procured."[53] Occasionally he cast a vote, descending briefly from his Olympian perch, then resumed his high place. Most of the time he stood forth as a neutral arbiter and honest broker.

Although highly intelligent, Washington lacked a philosophical mind that could originate constitutional ideas. John Adams once observed that the founding generation had "been sent into life at a time when the greatest lawgivers of antiquity would have wished to live," but this particular brand of greatness eluded George Washington.[54] It is hard to picture him springing to his feet in debate or remonstrating over an issue. He was doubtless content to be consigned to the sidelines and contributed little during the debates. At the same time he lent the proceedings his tacit blessing, allowing others to act as architects of the new order. He embodied the public excluded from the secret proceedings, and his mere presence reassured Americans that the delegates were striving for the public good instead of hatching a secret cabal behind closed doors.

As convention president, Washington assumed a dignified and sometimes severe air. William Pierce of Georgia recounted how one day a delegate dropped a copy of some proposed resolutions. This paper was brought to Washington, who was appalled that someone had so carelessly threatened the secrecy of the deliberations. He promptly rose to chastise the delegates and, as always, had a knack for projecting suppressed wrath: "Gentlemen, I am sorry to find that some one member of this body has been so neglectful of the secrets of the convention as to drop in the State House a copy of their proceedings, which by accident was picked up and delivered to me this morning. I must entreat [the] gentlemen to be more careful, lest our transactions get into the newspapers and disturb the public repose by premature speculations." He tossed the paper onto the table before him. "I do not know whose paper it is, but there it is—let him who owns it take it."[55] Washington donned his hat and strode angrily from the room. Momentarily unable to find his own copy, Pierce crept to the rostrum with some trepidation and was relieved to see someone else's handwriting on the paper. In the end, nobody had the nerve to claim it and confront Washington. The vignette shows how Washington functioned as the conscience of the convention and could make this room full of dignitaries feel like guilty schoolboys, summoned to the headmaster's office for a reprimand.

Washington paid such strict heed to the convention's secrecy rule that, even in his diary, he refrained from recording developments, limiting himself to saying, "Attended convention as usual." Otherwise he drew a discreet veil across the proceedings, dwelling on his social activities. In correspondence, however, he drummed up support for the convention's work, telling Jefferson that the central government had virtually ceased to function and that "unless a remedy is soon applied, anarchy and confusion will inevitably ensue."[56]

A story told of Washington at Philadelphia that may be apocryphal highlights several truths about his relations with his colleagues. One evening some Continental Army veterans were discussing the general's aloofness and the way he communicated to people that he didn't like to be touched or treated familiarly. Gouverneur Morris, dismissing this as nonsense, said he could be as familiar with Washington as with anyone else. Alexander Hamilton proposed a wager: he would buy dinner for a dozen delegates if Morris strode up to Washington, gave him a friendly slap on the shoulder, and said, "My dear General, how happy I am to see you look so well."[57] Morris tried the experiment—and Washington turned and fixed him with an icy glare that made Morris regret his error.

The convention sessions, which ran from ten A.M. to four P.M. daily, left considerable time for delegates to tour the city. Wherever Washington went, he was treated as a head of state, and people flocked after him. "In 1775, we beheld him at the head of the armies of America, arresting the progress of British tyranny," intoned the *Pennsylvania Gazette*. "In the year 1787, we behold him at the head of a chosen band of patriots and heroes, arresting the progress of American anarchy."[58] When a local resident, Jacob Hiltzheimer, tried to sneak a peek at the hero at close range, he found him swallowed up in large crowds. "In the evening [of June 4]," he wrote, "my wife and I went to Market Street gate to see that great and good man, General Washington. We had a full view of him and Major [William] Jackson, who walked with him, but the number of people who followed him on all sides was astonishing."[59]

Perhaps hoping to flee the crowds, Washington rose early in the morning and took brisk rides with his slave and coachman Giles. Spotted all over Philadelphia with his slaves, Washington made sure they were suitably dressed for the national stage, especially Billy Lee. Two days after arriving, Washington went on a special shopping expedition to get soap powder, a puff, and a black silk handkerchief for

Lee; a month later he bought him two pairs of stockings and a pair of breeches. The chief consideration was surely that Lee should reflect credit on his master, but one wonders whether Washington felt any extra gratitude for the services Lee had rendered in the Continental Army. It would also be intriguing to know whether Lee, Paris, and Giles lingered outside the State House as Washington and the other delegates debated inside the meaning of freedom and the fate of slavery in America.

CHAPTER FORTY-FOUR

Rising Sun

For most of the convention, Washington sat in splendid isolation at the front. On May 29, when Edmund Randolph presented the Virginia Plan, the convention reverted to a committee of the whole, and Nathaniel Gorham temporarily supplanted Washington in the presidential chair. After June 19 Washington resumed his place in the high seat that previewed his future status in the federal government. In the early days in Philadelphia he was heartened by the seeming harmony among the delegates, telling George Augustine that "the sentiments of the different members seem to accord more than I expected they would, as far as we have yet gone."[1] The general contours of the system that Jay and Madison had sketched out for him—a tripartite government, with a bicameral legislature—enlisted general support. Nonetheless, sharp clashes soon emerged, especially on the explosive issue of representation. On June 6 James Madison spoke in favor of direct election to the House of Representatives, based on proportional representation—a position supported by the populous states—and conjured up a vision of a broad, pluralistic republic. In mid-June William Paterson of New Jersey, champion of the smaller states, countered with a plan that foresaw states represented equally in Congress. Though mute on the podium, Washington supported Madison's view.

Fueled by the apprehensions of smaller states, the amity celebrated by Washington in early June had crumbled by the end of the month. On June 30, the weather having grown sweltering, Gunning Bedford of Delaware delivered a hot-tempered tirade, aimed at the larger states, demonstrating just how bruising the discourse had become. "I do not, gentlemen, trust you," he told them. He even hinted at secession, saying apropos of the smaller states that "sooner than be ruined, there are foreign powers who will take us by the hand."[2] Washington and Madison gazed in dismay as their worst fears of disunion threatened to materialize before their eyes. In early July a disappointed Alexander Hamilton returned temporarily to New York on business and dropped a pessimistic note to Washington, saying how "seriously and deeply distressed" he was by the convention's divisive sniping: "I fear that we shall let slip the golden opportunity of rescuing the American empire from disunion, anarchy, and misery."[3] Hostile to new federal powers, the two other New York delegates, Robert Yates and John Lansing, Jr., left the convention by July 5, never to return.

Although he held his tongue during the debates, Washington was never a neutral party, and the interminable squabbling only reinforced his view that the country needed a potent central government to override the selfish ambitions of local politicians. The man associated with so many triumphs shuddered at the prospect of being associated with public failure. "I *almost* despair of seeing a favorable issue to . . . the convention and do therefore repent having had any agency in the business," he informed Hamilton on July 10, chastising "narrow-minded politicians . . . under the influence of local views."[4] In a gentle, almost fatherly way, he begged Hamilton, the prodigal son, to return to the fold. "I am sorry you went away," he said. "I wish you were back. The crisis is equally important and alarming and no opposition under such circumstances should discourage exertions till the signature is fixed."[5]

While the convention dragged on, Washington drank enormous quantities of tea at the City Tavern and the Indian Queen, two haunts frequented by delegates. In his social life, he exhibited expert political instincts and embraced a wide spectrum of citizens, as if he already saw the presidency looming dimly on the horizon. On one of his first Sundays, he attended a Roman Catholic mass and also dined with Mark Prager, Sr., a Jewish merchant. On several occasions he joined fraternal dinners hosted by the Irish American Sons of St. Patrick. In early June he yielded to the importunate General Mifflin and reviewed the infantry, cavalry, and artillery of Philadelphia, as if he were already more than merely president of the convention.

Washington's Philadelphia itineraries reflected his far-ranging interests. Surgeon Abraham Chovet gave him a private tour of his Anatomical Museum, with its ingenious displays of human figures. Washington also gratified his abiding love of theater by catching plays at the Southwark Theater, which lay beyond Philadelphia's borders because of a law banning theater performances in the city proper. He evinced continuing solicitude for artists, sitting for an engraving by Charles Willson Peale and a portrait by Robert Edge Pine, who needed to touch up work begun at Mount Vernon two years earlier. In his wanderings, he visited a gristmill on the Schuylkill River and exhausted the proprietor with questions. "This day, Gen. Washington, Gen. Mifflin and four others of the convention did us the honor of paying us a visit in order to see our vineyard and bee houses," said Peter Legaux, a French immigrant. "In this they found great delight, asked a number of questions, and testified their highest approbation with my manner of managing bees."[6] At Franklin's house, Washington revealed a sharp interest in mechanical inventions, marveling at a mangle used for pressing items after they were washed.

As always, Washington's silences were as eloquent at his pronouncements. In late July he accompanied Robert Morris on a trout-fishing expedition to a creek near Valley Forge, prompting him to ride over to his old army cantonment. In his diary, Washington mentioned having "visited all the works, which were in ruins, and the encampments in woods, where the ground had not been cultivated."[7] When he last saw Valley Forge, it had been cold and gloomy, bare of all foliage. Now it was a balmy place, lush with summer greenery. The sight undoubtedly stirred deep-seated memories in Washington, but his diary entry for that day is curiously reticent; even by Washingtonian standards, it is a gem of emotional evasion. After a one-sentence allusion to Valley Forge, he continued, "On my return back to Mrs. Moore's, observing some farmers at work and entering into conversation with them, I received the following information with respect to the mode of cultivating buckwheat and the application of the grain."[8] He then listed various ways to sow, plow, and harrow buckwheat, as if that were the day's major occurrence. On some level, Washington felt the powerful lure of the past yet could never articulate it. He proved only a touch more expansive after visiting the site of the Germantown battle, stating that he had "contemplated on the dangers which threatened the American Army at that place."[9] That was his total commentary. Active and forward-looking, Washington did not amble very often down memory lane, though some dinner guests at Mount Vernon recalled him reminiscing about the war.

In the absence of Martha's company, Washington continued to gravitate toward alluring female society. When he dined at a club composed of the city's leading gentlemen, he noted that they invited female family members on alternate Saturdays. Not surprisingly, Washington chose that day to attend, specifying, "This was the ladies day."[10] Several times he called upon Elizabeth Powel and dusted off a musty streak of gallantry. As he wrote to her on July 23, "Gen[era]l Washington presents his respectful compliments to Mrs. Powel and will do himself the honor of calling upon her at or before 5 o'clock (in his carriage) in hopes of the pleasure of conducting her to Lansdown this evening."[11] From the chivalrous tone of these messages, one senses that Washington could sometimes enjoy flirtatious banter. A week later, noting his trout-fishing trip to the Valley Forge area, he declined an invitation to escort Mrs. Powel to a performance of Sheridan's *School for Scandal*: "The Gen[era]l can but regret that matters have turned out so unluckily after waiting so long to receive a lesson in the School for Scandal."[12] Washington seldom allowed himself the liberty of jesting with a married lady in this manner. His lighthearted tone with Elizabeth Powel makes one wonder anew about the role of repressed sexuality in George Washington's life. We have no evidence that he ever talked to Martha in this coy manner, nor is it easy to imagine. For all the happiness of their marriage, Martha had become his life's standard prose while Elizabeth Powel, like Sally Fairfax, may have introduced some forbidden spice of poetry. It was as if, during his extended sojourn in Philadelphia, the footloose Washington permitted himself to explore sides of his personality that he kept firmly under wraps at home.

NOT LONG AFTER Washington wrote so gloomily to Hamilton, the Constitutional Convention experienced a spectacular breakthrough. In mid-July it was agreed that the small states would be represented equally in the Senate, while the House would have proportional representation based on population. For Washington and other Virginia delegates, it was a bitter pill to swallow, threatening to weaken the federal government critically. Nonetheless, an eminently pragmatic man, Washington accepted the need for painful compromises to form a union, assuring Henry Knox that the government being shaped by the delegates was "the best that can be obtained at the present moment, under such diversity of ideas as prevail."[13]

Perhaps the most uncomfortable debate hinged on the slavery issue. The abolitionist movement had made considerable headway in New England but was losing ground in the South after a brief flurry of postwar interest. Slavery was the most vexing topic at the convention. As Pierce Butler of South Carolina commented, "The security the southern states want is that their negroes may not be taken from them, which some gentlemen within or without doors have a very good mind to do."[14] Employing thinly disguised blackmail, some southern delegates vowed to quit the convention if anyone interfered with their peculiar institution. "The true question at present is whether the southern states shall, or shall not, be parties to the union," said John Rutledge of South Carolina.[15]

The delegates agreed that slavery wouldn't be mentioned by name in the Constitution, giving way to transparent euphemisms, such as "persons held to service or labor." Slaveholders won some substantial concessions. For the purposes of representation in the House of Representatives and the Electoral College, they would be able to count three-fifths of their slave population. This was no mean feat: slaves made up 40 percent of the population in Virginia, for instance, and 60 percent in South Carolina. The slave trade would also be shielded from any tampering for at least twenty years. Through a fugitive slave clause, masters would be able to reclaim runaway slaves in free states—a provision George Washington would liberally employ in future years. Referring to these hard-fought victories for the southern states, the abolitionist William Lloyd Garrison would later castigate the Constitution as "a covenant with death and an agreement with hell."[16]

Whatever his own nascent abolitionist views, George Washington wasn't about to make an open stand at the convention and joined other delegates in daydreaming that slavery would fade away at some nebulous future date. Isolated critics branded Washington a hypocrite for clinging to his slaves after a revolution fought in the name of freedom. At the Massachusetts convention that ratified the Constitution, one speaker deplored his status as a slaveholder. "Oh, Washington, what a name he has had! How he has immortalized himself!" he exclaimed, then remarked that Washington "holds those in slavery who have as good a right to be free as he has. He is still for self and, in my opinion, his character has sunk 50 percent."[17] A Massachusetts newspaper, echoing this charge, regretted that Washington had "wielded the sword in defense of American liberty yet at the same time, was, and is to this day, living upon the labors of several hundreds of miserable Africans as freeborn as himself."[18]

The debate over the executive branch was likewise steeped in controversy. Delegates had difficulty conceiving a mighty presidency that did not look suspiciously like a monarchy, and they trod gingerly in this treacherous territory. The idea of a separate executive branch with a president independent of the legislature and able to veto its laws was regarded as heretical in some quarters. Benjamin Franklin so distrusted executive power that he pushed for a small executive council instead of a president. In advancing this idea, he had the courtesy to note, with a figurative nod toward Washington, that the first president would likely be benevolent, but he feared despotic tendencies in his successors.

That the delegates overcame their dread of executive power and produced an energetic presidency can be traced directly to Washington's imperturbable presence. Pierce Butler doubted that the presidential powers would have been so great "had not many members cast their eyes toward General Washington as president and shaped their ideas of the powers to a president by their opinion of his virtue."[19] As convention president, Washington sat through extensive discussions of what was turning into his job description. There was a tacit assumption that, the office having been conceived with him in mind, Washington would serve as the first president. With his image before their eyes, the delegates were inevitably governed by their hopes instead of their fears. Still, with memories of the Revolution fresh, they reserved significant powers for Congress, endowing it, for instance, with the authority to declare war, thereby avoiding the British precedent of a monarch who retained this awesome power.

For all his inscrutable silence, Washington disclosed specific views several times during the convention. When Elbridge Gerry proposed a constitutional limit of three thousand men in any standing army, Washington supposedly remarked drily that "no foreign enemy should invade the United States, at any time, with more than three thousand troops."[20] At the end of the convention, he also took a decidedly democratic stand on the question of how many people each congressman should represent, opting for thirty thousand instead of forty thousand to ensure "security for the rights and interests of the people."[21] Blessed by Washington, the convention adopted this change unanimously, in a striking instance of his irresistible appeal. That Washington was an exponent of an energetic presidency was also evident when he voted for requiring a three-fourths majority in Congress to override a presidential veto. Despite Washington's backing, it was reduced to a two-thirds majority to forestall abuses of executive power.

Whatever pleasure he derived from being away from Mount Vernon had disappeared by September 9, when he wrote to George Augustine that the convention would likely wind up its deliberations within a week: "God grant I may not be disappointed in this expectation, as I am quite homesick."[22] The long hours and sedentary job must have proved an ordeal for him. A day earlier the convention had convened a committee on style, with Gouverneur Morris as its head, to give the Constitution its finished form. The foppish, peg-legged Morris was a delightful bon vivant with considerable verbal resources who relished Washington's "cool, steady temper."[23] Washington, in turn, enjoyed Morris's lively flow of quips, his "first-rate abilities," and his "lively and brilliant imagination."[24] It was Morris who drafted the great preamble to the Constitution that began with the memorable flourish "We the People." On September 12 delegates received printed copies of the final document, and as he led them through it, Washington personally inserted the changes that had been approved while the committee on style was hard at work.

Whatever his misgivings about individual provisions, Washington was no lukewarm supporter of the final document. As he later expressed it, the Constitution was "the result of a spirit of amity and mutual concession" and more coherent than anyone had a right to expect from so many discordant delegates with passionate opinions.[25] It struck him as "little short of a miracle," he told Lafayette, that "delegates from so many different states . . . should unite in forming a system of national government so little liable to well-founded objections."[26] In another letter he said, "It approached nearer to perfection than any government hitherto instituted among men."[27] Especially sensitive to allegations that the president was vested with excessive power, he stressed the numerous safeguards put in place, telling Lafayette that the new constitution "is provided with more checks and barriers against the introduction of tyranny . . . than any government" previously devised by mortals.[28] As president, Washington went so far as to say that the "invisible hand" of providence had been manifest in the enactment of the Constitution.[29]

In correspondence Washington admitted to imperfections in the new charter but trusted to the amendment process to refine it. The Constitutional Convention was no conclave of sages in Roman togas, handing down eternal truths engraved in marble, and he wondered how long the document would last. He parted company with Edmund Randolph, who refused to sign the Constitution unless it provided for a second convention to enact necessary amendments. For Washington, the beauty of the document was that it charted a path for its own evolution. Its very brevity and generality—it contained fewer than eight thousand words—meant it would be a constantly changing document, susceptible to shifting interpretations. It would be left to Washington and other founders to convert this succinct, deliberately vague statement into a working reality. He also knew that the American public needed to contribute its share; the Constitution "can only lay the foundation—the community at large must raise the edifice."[30] Benjamin Franklin shared this view. Legend claims that as he left the State House, Franklin bumped into Elizabeth Powel, who inquired about the form of government produced inside. "A republic, madam, if you can keep it," Franklin replied.[31] Powel later claimed that she had no recollection of the famous retort, but she did say that "the most respectable, influential members of the convention" had gathered at her house and that "the all important subject was frequently discussed" there.[32]

On Monday, September 17, 1787, the convention's last day, the delegates adopted the Constitution "unanimously," although there was poetic license in the use of the word. It had taken four long months to attain this historic agreement. After starting out with 55 delegates—all of them white and male, and many affluent—the convention had suffered a high rate of attrition, with only 42 present at the end; of those, 39 signed the document. Eleven states approved the Constitution; Alexander Hamilton signed individually as the sole remaining delegate from New York. Rhode Island had boycotted the convention altogether. To Madison, Washington explained how important "the appearance of unanimity" was in presenting the Constitution to Congress: "Not everyone has opportunities to peep behind the curtain, and as the multitude often judge from externals, the appearance of unanimity in that body, on this occas[io]n, will be of great importance."[33] It was a telling comment from a man who placed a premium on political stagecraft.

Of the three convention holdouts, two came from Virginia—Edmund Randolph and George Mason—and happened to be close friends of Washington; the third was Elbridge Gerry of Massachusetts. As heir apparent to the presidency, Washington undoubtedly took offense when Mason declared that the new government "would end either in monarchy or a tyrannical aristocracy" and complained that the Constitution "had been formed without the knowledge . . . of the people."[34] Their thirty-year friendship did not survive their heated split. "Col. Mason left

Philad[elphi]a in an exceeding ill humor," Madison afterward told Washington. "He returned to Virginia with a fixed disposition to prevent the adoption of the plan if possible. He considers the want of a Bill of Rights as a fatal objection."[35] The convention's secrecy rule deplored by Mason had stimulated candor but was immediately blasted by critics and engendered a thousand conspiracy theories. "I am sorry they began their deliberations by so abominable a precedent as that of tying up the tongues of their members," Jefferson complained to John Adams.[36] To guarantee confidentiality, William Jackson, the convention secretary, burned all loose scraps of paper and entrusted the official journals to George Washington's care—another act of tremendous faith in his integrity.

On the final day, Benjamin Franklin mentioned to some delegates that during the previous months he had often stared at the presidential chair in which Washington sat with its image of the sun: "I have often and often in the course of the session . . . looked at that [sun] behind the president without being able to tell whether it was rising or setting. But now at length I have the happiness to know that it is a rising and not a setting sun."[37] After Franklin dispensed this famous aperçu, the delegates adjourned to the City Tavern for one last round of drinks. In sending the Constitution to Congress, Washington wisely made an understated case for approval, noting the conciliatory spirit that had led to its passage: "That it will meet the full and entire approbation of every state is not perhaps to be expected . . . That it is liable to as few exceptions as could reasonably have been expected, we hope and believe."[38]

On September 18, accompanied by John Blair of Virginia, Washington boarded his newly varnished coach and set out for Mount Vernon. The two men traveled in high style, Washington having refurbished his vehicle in Philadelphia, outfitting it with glass panes, brass plates, stuffed cushions, and a new carpet. In his eagerness to return home, he was misled into an uncharacteristic error. Near the Head of Elk he had to ford a river swollen by torrential rains. Instead of waiting for the turbulent waters to subside, the overly eager Washington decided to take the carriage across an "old, rotten, and long disused" bridge, as he described it.[39] One of the two harnessed horses suddenly slid off the bridge and nearly dragged the other horse, along with the baggage-laden carriage, into the foaming waters. Only the prompt intervention of some nearby millers, who managed to disengage the first horse from its harness, prevented the total destruction of the carriage and Washington's belongings.

At sunset on September 22 Washington's coach pulled up before the mansion house at Mount Vernon. That he was ready to resume his everyday life is evident in his diary, where he jotted down his absence of "four months and 14 days."[40] The precision of detail suggests how onerous Washington considered the lost time, and he bewailed to a correspondent having "sacrificed every private consideration and personal enjoyment" to attend the convention.[41] What he discovered upon return-ing home confirmed his latent anxieties about his neglected business affairs. As he told Henry Knox, he "found Mrs. Washington and the family tolerably well, but the fruits of the earth almost entirely destroyed by one of the severest droughts (in this neighborhood) that ever was experienced. The crops generally below the mountains are injured, but not to the degree that mine and some of my neighbors' are here."[42] For Washington, this dispiriting discovery reenacted a now-familiar tale of making huge private sacrifices whenever he was forced to be away from home for public service.

CHAPTER FORTY-FIVE

Mounting the Seat

THE CONSTITUTION cherished by generations of Americans was fiercely controversial at first, producing heated polemics on both sides. So that its legitimacy would derive from the people, not the state governments, the framers required ratification by a special convention in each state; the document would be activated when nine states approved. By all accounts, Washington overflowed with enthusiasm for the new charter. When Richmond merchant Alexander Donald stayed at Mount Vernon in early October 1787, he was impressed by Washington's ebullient advocacy. "I never saw him so keen for anything in my life as he is for the adoption of a new form of government," Donald informed Jefferson.[1] The months in Philadelphia, however trying, had given Washington a needed respite from business worries and revived his faltering health. "He is in perfect good health," Donald wrote, "and looks almost as well as he did twenty years ago."[2]

Everybody recognized the signal importance of Washington's imprimatur on the new charter, reassuring a public skittish about such fundamental change. His cachet emboldened advocates (called federalists) even as it undermined critics (called antifederalists). "I have observed that your name [attached] to the new constitution has been of infinite service," Gouverneur Morris wrote. "Indeed, I am convinced that, if you had not attended the convention and the same paper had been handed out to the world, it would have met with a colder reception . . . As it is, should the idea prevail that you would not accept of the presidency, it would prove fatal in many parts."[3]

One Boston newspaper regretted that the combined prestige of Washington and Franklin in favor of the Constitution made "too strong an argument in the minds of many to suffer them to examine, like freemen, for themselves."[4] Some antifederalists took refuge in hyperbole, portraying the Constitutional Convention as a baleful nest of conspirators—a charge given some resonance by the secret nature of the proceedings. "The evil genius of darkness presided at its birth; it came forth under the veil of mystery," wrote an opponent who styled himself "Centinel."[5] That Washington and Franklin had mingled among those conspirators made it more difficult to defame the enterprise. To bypass this problem, "Centinel" depicted Washington as an unwitting tool of "aspiring despots" who were "prostituting the name of a Washington to cloak their designs upon your liberties."[6] Washington dismissed such conspiracy theories as preposterous: "At my age and in my circumstances, what sinister object or personal emolument had I to seek after in this life?"[7]

After a pleasing October visit from Elizabeth and Samuel Powel, Washington had to cope with another frigid winter at Mount Vernon. Severed from the outside world by snow, he stayed in touch by mail with federalists in many states. Resigning himself to a common eighteenth-century practice, he assumed that his letters would be opened, telling Lafayette, "As to my sentiments with respect to the merits of the new constitution, I will disclose them without reserve (although by passing through the post offices they should become known to all the world) for, in truth, I have nothing to conceal on that subject."[8]

While preserving an air of Olympian detachment, Washington moved stealthily in the background of the ratification process, one of his chief worries being that the Constitution's detractors would prove more adept than its advocates. Although he admitted to defects in the charter, he tended to regard supporters as righteous and reasonable, opponents as wrongheaded and duplicitous. As a stalwart realist, he thought it dangerous to demand perfection from any human production and questioned "the propriety of preventing men from doing good, because there is a possibility of their doing evil."[9] When Lieutenant John Enys stopped by Mount Vernon in February, Washington explained that he had followed doggedly the constitutional debates, consuming all the pertinent literature. "He said he had read with attention every publication," Enys wrote, "both for and against it, in order to see whether there could be any new objections, or that it could be placed in any other light than what it had been in the general convention, for which . . . he said he had sought in vain."[10]

New York quickly emerged as a major locus of dissent, and Madison, based there as a delegate in the waning days of the Confederation Congress, warned Washington of a powerful backlash gathering force: "The newspapers here begin to teem with vehement and virulent calumniations of the proposed gov[ernmen]t."[11] After leaving the convention in July, Hamilton had fired anonymous salvos in the New York press against Governor George Clinton, who felt threatened by centralized power. On September 20 the Clinton forces retaliated with vicious glee, accusing Hamilton of insinuating himself into Washington's good graces during the war. Said the nameless critic: "I have also known an upstart attorney palm himself upon a great and good man, for a youth of extraordinary genius and, under the shadow of such a patronage, make himself at once known and respected. But . . . he was at length found to be a superficial, self-conceited coxcomb and was of course turned off and disregarded by his patron."[12] This remark hatched an enduring mythology of a wily Hamilton tricking the dunderheaded Washington into supporting him.

Distraught over these accusations, the hypersensitive Hamilton appealed to Washington to rebut the notion that he had imposed himself upon the commander in chief and had then been dismissed by him: "This, I confess, hurts my feelings and, if it obtains credit, will require a contradiction."[13] By return mail, Washington laid both falsehoods to rest: "With respect to the first, I have no cause to believe that you took a single step to accomplish [it] or had the most distant [ide]a of receiving an appointment in my [fam]ily till you were invited thereto. And [with] respect to the second . . . your quitting [it was] altogether the effect of your own [choic]e."[14]

To combat vocal foes of the Constitution in New York, Hamilton published in late October the first essay of *The Federalist* under the pen name "Publius" and rushed a copy to Washington. Washington had told David Humphreys that the Constitution's acceptance would depend upon "the recommendation of it by good pens," and *The Federalist* must have seemed a case of answered prayers.[15] Indeed, the federalists possessed the preponderance of literary talent. "For the remaining numbers of Publius," Washington informed Hamilton, "I shall acknowledge myself obliged, as I am persuaded the subject will be well handled by the author."[16] The perceptive Washington saw that *The Federalist* transcended journalism and would take on classic status, telling Hamilton that "when the transient circumstances and fugitive performances which attended this crisis shall have disappeared, that work will merit the notice of posterity."[17]

In November, when Madison sent Washington the first seven installments of *The Federalist,* he admitted in confidence to being one of its unnamed authors and urged Washington to convey the essays to influential Virginians who might get them published. Without tipping his hand, Washington became a secret partner in the *Federalist* enterprise, transmitting the essays to David Stuart in Richmond. "Altho[ugh] I am acquainted with some of the writers who are concerned in this work," wrote Washington, playing things close to the vest, "I am not at liberty to disclose their names, nor would I have it known that they are sent by *me* to *you* for promulgation."[18] To maintain the flow of reprints in Virginia, Madison sent Washington packets of new *Federalist* essays and bound editions as they appeared. Curiously, Washington had not figured out that John Jay was the third member of the *Federalist* triumvirate. When a letter appeared in a Baltimore paper announcing that Jay had denounced the Constitution as "a wicked conspiracy," Madison had to reassure Washington that the letter was "an arrant forgery."[19] In March, Henry Knox finally let the cat out of the bag: "The publication signed *Publius* is attributed to the joint efforts of Mr. Jay, Mr. Madison and Colo. Hamilton."[20]

By mid-January 1788 the Constitution had been adopted by decisive margins in Pennsylvania, New Jersey, Delaware, Georgia, and Connecticut. These early victories were deceptive, however, for closely contested state conventions lay ahead. The most formidable opposition, Washington surmised, would be marshaled in New York and Virginia. As the biggest, richest, and most populous state, Virginia had to be the linchpin of any union. While he believed that most Virginians stood four-square behind the Constitution, Washington conceded the influential nature of its opponents, especially George Mason, Edmund Randolph, and Patrick Henry, who he feared would stoop to demagoguery. With these dissenting delegates, Washington engaged in low-key lobbying, telling Randolph that the new charter was "the best constitution that can be contained at this epoch and that this or a dissolution of the union . . . are the only alternatives before us."[21] In a sign of subtle disenchantment with Virginia, Washington observed that it was "a little strange that the men of large property in the south should be more afraid that the constitution should produce an aristocracy or a monarchy than the genuine democratical people of the east."[22] It is hard not to see a veiled criticism of southern slavery behind this comment.

As he awaited its convention, Washington knew that, if Virginia failed to join the union, he would be ineligible for the presidency. After the first five states voted for the Constitution, political wrangling intensified over the future leadership of the impending government. In Massachusetts, scheduled to hold the sixth ratifying convention, federalists tried to woo a wavering John Hancock by promising to support him for vice president if Washington ran for president. They also intimated that, if Virginia didn't ratify and Washington couldn't run for president, they would line up solidly behind Hancock for the top job.

By May, Massachusetts, Maryland, and South Carolina had also ratified the Constitution, bringing the total to eight states, one short of the magic number needed to enact it. This put additional pressure on the states that were about to hold their conventions. Washington followed the cascading victories with mounting excitement. "The plot thickens fast," he told Lafayette. "A few short weeks will determine the political fate of America for the present generation and probably produce no small influence on the happiness of society through a long succession of ages to come."[23]

In early June, as Washington visited his "aged and infirm mother" in Fredericksburg, national attention turned to the Virginia Ratifying Convention.[24] Though he was ailing and felt "extremely feeble," James Madison delivered astounding oratory on behalf of the new charter.[25] Washington's nephew Bushrod, awed by Madison's talents, reported to Mount Vernon that Madison had spoken "with such force of reasoning and a display of such irresistible truths that opposition seemed to have quitted the field."[26] In a pivotal shift, Governor Randolph capitulated and teamed up with the federalists from fear that Virginia would be ostracized if it didn't ratify. This argument gained additional currency when New Hampshire became the ninth state to ratify and ended all suspense about the Constitution's future. Still unaware of what had happened in New England, Virginia four days later approved the Constitution by a ten-vote margin. In late July New York became the eleventh state to sign on, leaving only Rhode Island and North Carolina beyond the pale of union. Not until June 28 did Washington receive news of the Virginia and New Hampshire victories. He must have known that these tidings would carry in their wake an insistent plea for him to become the first president. In backing the new charter, Washington had waged an enormous high-stakes campaign, and his prestige soared even higher with its enactment. "Be assured [Washington's] influence carried this government," declared James Monroe.[27]

The town of Alexandria blazed with lights in celebration of the Constitution as the news ricocheted up and down the Potomac by precisely timed discharges of cannon. When Washington rode to Alexandria for a festive dinner, he "was met some miles out of town by a party of gentlemen on horseback and escorted to the tavern, having been saluted on his way by the light infantry company in a respectful manner," he told Charles Cotesworth Pinckney.[28] On June 3 he welcomed the triumphant Madison back to Mount Vernon but found him worn down by the tremendous campaign he had conducted. With paternal delicacy, Washington advised the younger man "to take a little respite from business" and linger at Mount Vernon: "Moderate exercise and books occasionally, with the mind unbent, will be your best restoratives." He coaxed the harried Madison into staying for four days, during which time the two men remained in seclusion for many hours, discussing practical details of the upcoming government.

With the Constitution having squeaked by in Virginia, George Washington owed an incalculable debt to Madison for making his presidency possible. Some Virginia foes of the new charter reacted graciously in defeat. By shifting ground, Edmund Randolph had redeemed his political future, later telling Washington that "the constitution would never have been adopted, but from a knowledge that you had once sanctified it and an expectation that you would execute it."[29] Quite different was the obstinacy of George Mason, which provoked a caustic aside from Washington: "Pride on the one hand and want of manly candor on the other will not, I am certain, let him acknowledge an error in his opinions . . . though conviction should flash on his mind as strongly as a ray of light."[30] What bothered Washington was less Mason's opposition than his bullheaded rigidity. Of Mason's followers, he said, "They are in the habit of thinking that everything he says and does is right and (if capable) they will not judge for themselves."[31] As later became clear, George Washington refused to appoint anyone to the new government who had been overtly hostile to the Constitution that brought it into being.

Once the Constitution was adopted, Washington could not evade the question of whether he would serve as president. He stood in a league of his own, his stature inimitable. Like other founders, he regarded any open interest in power as unbecoming to a gentleman. As a result, he preferred to be drawn reluctantly from private life by the irresistible summons of public service. He eschewed the word *president,* as if merely saying it might connote an unsavory desire on his part. As with attending the Constitutional Convention, he again worried that people would think he had yielded to the allure of worldly pomp and had cynically broken his pledge not to return to public life. His usual besetting fears of failure also reemerged. Years later, chatting confidentially with Madison, Washington recalled that "he had from the beginning found himself deficient in many of the essential qualifications [for president], owing to his inexperience in the forms of public business, his unfitness to judge of legal questions and questions arising out of the constitution."[32] Once again he was preoccupied with presumed taunts and criticisms, the inner voice of his own unspoken fears.

For both political and psychological reasons, Washington needed to undergo a protracted period of indecision about the presidency. Part of him felt genuinely burdened by public life, especially since he experienced "the increasing infirmities of nature," as he told Lafayette.[33] He was torn, as always, by unacknowledged ambition mingled with self-doubt. During his October visit to Mount Vernon, Alexander Donald felt that Washington's pro forma denial of interest in the presidency masked his true feelings. "As the eyes of all America are turned towards this truly great and good man for the first president, I took the liberty of sounding him upon it," Donald told Jefferson. "He appears to be greatly against going into public life again, pleads in excuse for himself his love of retirement and his advanced age. But, notwithstanding of these, I am fully of opinion he may be induced to appear once more on the public stage of life."[34]

Having been lionized for renouncing power at the war's end, Washington found it hard to concede normal human ambition. In the *Columbian Magazine* of November 1787, a poet calling himself "Cinna" wrote rapturous verses that cast him in superhuman terms. Evoking the universal fraud and avarice of a corrupt age, "Cinna" held forth Washington as the rare exception, the man "Whom boundless trust ne'er tempted to betray, / Nor power impelled to arbitrary sway."[35] Such idolatry made it difficult for Washington to be truthful about his feelings. He also had to reckon with heightened paranoia after the convention, a widespread apprehension that the new president might transform himself into a king. The only way he could proceed, it seemed, was to show extreme reluctance to become president, then be swept along by others.

As his name was bruited about for president, Washington was caught in an excruciating predicament. Merely to broach the topic, even in strict confidence with friends, might seem to betray some secret craving on his part. As he later confessed to Hamilton, he dared not seek advice: "For situated as I am, I could hardly bring the question into the slightest discussion, or ask an opinion, even in the most confidential manner, without betraying, in my judgment, some impropriety of conduct."[36] For this reason he must have been grateful to friends who talked to him forthrightly about the presidency. A month after Washington left Philadelphia, Gouverneur Morris told him that among the "thirteen horses now about to be coupled together, there are some of every race and character. They will listen to your voice and submit to your control. You therefore must, I say, *must* mount this seat."[37] From abroad, Lafayette cheerfully added his voice to the chorus: "I beg you, my dear general, do not refuse the responsibility of the presidency during the first few years. You alone can make this political machine operate successfully."[38] This was a powerful argument for Washington, who had gone to Philadelphia feeling that the war would be incomplete without a new Constitution; now, he knew, the Constitution would be incomplete without an effective new government.

Perhaps the most subtly persuasive pleas emanated from Hamilton, who could easily picture himself holding a significant place in a Washington administration. He stalked Washington for the presidency with all the cunning at his disposal, piling up every good, unselfish reason for running. In mid-August 1788 he wrote to Washington and introduced the forbidden subject but never used the word *president*. He presented the first presidency as the logical, nay inevitable, sequel to the Constitutional Convention for Washington: "You will permit me to say that it is indispensable you should lend yourself to [the new government's] first operations. It is to little purpose to have *introduced* a system, if the weightiest influence is not given to its firm *establishment* in the outset."[39] Washington had to undergo this ritual of spurning the proffered crown. "On the delicate subject with which you conclude your letter, I can say nothing," Washington replied. "For you know me well enough, my good Sir, to be persuaded that I am not guilty of affectation when I tell you, it is my great and sole desire to live and die, in peace and retirement, on my own farm . . . while you and some others who are acquainted with my heart would *acquit*, the world and posterity might probably *accuse* me of *inconsistency* and *am-*

bition.[40] So among those whose opinion Washington considered was posterity. He portrayed himself as paralyzed by indecision and referred to the "dreaded dilemma of being forced to accept or refuse" the presidency.[41] Whenever he mused about the problem, he told Hamilton, he "felt a kind of gloom upon my mind."[42]

As their exchanges continued, Hamilton upped the stakes, telling Washington he had no choice but to assume the presidency. Now older and more self-confident than the wartime aide-de-camp, Hamilton addressed Washington as a peer. The success of the new government was hardly self-evident, and only Washington, he argued, could put the new Constitution to a fair test. If the first government failed, "the framers of it will have to encounter the disrepute of having brought about a revolution in government, without substituting anything that was worthy of the effort."[43] Hamilton contended that Washington's refusal to become president would "throw everything into confusion."[44] This was what Washington yearned to hear: that overwhelming necessity demanded that he make the supreme sacrifice and serve as president.

Washington believed that the new government needed a fair trial and an auspicious start. He always credited the power of first impressions and now imagined that "the first transactions of a nation, like those of an individual upon his first entrance into life, make the deepest impression."[45] With Madison, he employed a powerful metaphor: "To be shipwrecked in sight of the port would be the severest of all possible aggravations to our misery."[46]

Beyond the image projected by the first government, also important was the fact that the first president, in conjunction with Congress, would shape its institutional structure. In Madison's words, the first two years would "produce all the great arrangements under the new system and . . . may fix its tone for a long time to come."[47] Washington knew this, but the prospect of such crushing responsibilities only intensified his dilemma. Having sat through the Constitutional Convention, he knew the sketchy nature of Article II, which dealt with the presidency: "I should consider myself as entering upon an unexplored field, enveloped on every side with clouds and darkness."[48] He also knew the presidency would convert him into a partisan figure, threatening his chaste reputation as the personification of America. In this vein, the *Federal Gazette* of Philadelphia worried that his wartime reputation would be blotted as he shifted from the "fields of military glory" into "the thorn-covered paths of political administration."[49]

The public clamor for Washington to become president arose from his heroism, his disinterested patriotism, and his willingness to surrender his wartime command. Another, if minor, factor was his apparent sterility and lack of children, which made it seem that he had been divinely preserved in an immaculate state to become the Father of His Country. In March 1788, in listing the arguments for electing Washington, the *Massachusetts Centinel* included this one: "As having no son—and therefore not exposing us to the danger of an hereditary successor."[50] This was a plausible fear at a time when monarchs routinely made dynastic marriages and when people worried that European powers would subvert the new republican government. John Adams expressed to Jefferson his relief that Washington would be a childless president: "If General Washington had a daughter, I firmly believe she would be demanded in marriage by one of the royal families of France or England, perhaps by both; or, if he had a son, he would be invited to come a courting to Europe."[51] To sway Washington to run, Gouverneur Morris slyly alluded to his childless state: "You will become the father to more than three millions of children."[52]

Assailed by doubts, Washington decided to serve only if convinced that "very disagreeable consequences" would result from his refusal.[53] As the election drew near, he made it plain that accepting the presidency would be his life's most painful decision. "Be assured, my dear sir," he told Lafayette, "I shall assume the task with the most unfeigned reluctance and with a real diffidence, for which I shall probably receive no credit from the world."[54] One way Washington reconciled himself to the job was to regard it as a temporary post that he would occupy only until the new government was established on a firm footing. In early October 1788 he confided to Hamilton that, if he became president, it would be with the hope "that at a convenient and an early period my services might be dispensed with and that I might be permitted once more to retire."[55] In fact, Washington later admitted to Jefferson that he had not planned to serve out a single term as president and had been "made to believe that in 2 years all would be well in motion and he might retire."[56] It seems safe to say that Washington never dreamed he would serve out even one full term as president, much less two. Had he realized that his decision would entangle him in eight more years of arduous service, he likely would never have agreed to be president.

The thing that, at a stroke, ended Washington's vacillation was the timetable set up by Congress for the election: presidential electors would be chosen in January 1789 and then vote in February. With his rather formal personality, Washington was lucky that he didn't need to engage in electioneering, for he lacked the requisite skills for such campaigning. Had he been forced to make speeches or debate on the stump, he would not have fared very well. Tailor-made for this transitional moment between the patrician style of the colonial past and the rowdy populism of the Jacksonian era, Washington could remain incommunicado as the electors voted.

In late January he was heartened by signs of a resounding victory for federalists in the first congressional elections, showing broad-gauged support for the Constitution. "I cannot help flattering myself [that] the new Congress on account of the . . . various talents of its members will not be inferior to any assembly in the world," he told Lafayette.[57] This would only have enhanced the presidency's attractions for Washington. If his election was predictable, it wasn't foreordained that he would win unanimously. In mid-January Henry Lee foresaw that even antifederalist electors would feel obliged to vote for Washington. Casting their votes on February 4, 1789, they vindicated Lee's prediction: all 69 electors voted for Washington, making him the only president in American history to win unanimously.

Lee also forecast with accuracy that the vote for vice president would be far more competitive. Under electoral rules then in force, each elector cast two ballots, the victor becoming president and the runner-up vice president. About the vice president, Washington remained studiously neutral, saying only that he would probably come from the powerful state of Massachusetts—which boiled down to a competition between John Adams and John Hancock. By early January Washington had heard that Adams was the likely choice, and he let it be known that he was "entirely satisfied with the arrangement for filling the second office," especially since it would forestall the election of an antifederalist.[58]

In retrospect, it seems certain that Washington would have outstripped Adams, but some were concerned that Adams might be popular enough in the northern states to edge out Washington as president. An unscrupulous campaign by antifederalists might sabotage Washington's candidacy by withholding votes for him. To prevent such a fiasco, Hamilton suggested privately to a few electors that they withhold votes from Adams to ensure Washington's victory. As it turned out, Hamilton's fears were grossly exaggerated: Washington's 69 votes far outpaced the 34 cast for Adams and 9 for John Jay. Vain and thin-skinned, Adams felt demeaned by receiving only half as many votes as Washington. Hamilton had not attempted to undercut Adams so much as to protect the presidency for Washington. Nonetheless, when Adams later learned of this covert campaign, he was outraged and faulted Hamilton for unconscionable duplicity, poisoning relations between the two men.

Supposed to assemble on March 4, the new Congress could not put together a quorum for another month. The reason for the delay spoke poorly for the country: the delegates had been hampered by the "extreme badness of the roads," Henry Knox informed Washington.[59] Confronted by many problems, the country could ill afford this anxious interregnum. It was a discouraging start, making America look like the backward nation of rude bumpkins derided by British Tories. Washington's election remained unofficial until the new Congress mustered a quorum in early April. Since a landslide victory for him was widely assumed, Washington would have been entitled to travel to New York for the opening of Congress. But detained by a punctilious regard for form, he refused to budge until Congress officially counted the votes on April 6. Things had proceeded much as Washington had wished: instead of seeming to clutch at power, he had let it descend slowly upon his shoulders, as if deposited there by the gentle hand of fate.

Just as Washington had renounced his salary as commander in chief of the Continental Army, so he tried to waive his presidential salary, but Congress insisted adamantly that he accept it. It proved a handsome $25,000 per annum compared to $5,000 for the vice president and $3,500 for the secretaries of state and treasury. Washington's desire to forgo a salary blended his past and present selves: he wanted to display his customary noblesse oblige and advertise his freedom from financial care, while also acting as the ideal public servant, devoid of mercenary motives. It was his way of emphasizing that he was less a professional politician than a gentleman graciously donating his time. In truth, Washington could not afford such magnanimity, and as he prepared for the presidency, he struggled to straighten out his disordered finances. He breathed not a word of his financial troubles to his political associates, who never knew of the handicaps he overcame.

From an economic standpoint, the period after Washington's return to Mount Vernon in December 1783 had been complicated by numerous setbacks. The persistent failure of his corn and wheat crops, thanks in part to a severe chinch bug infestation, had slashed his income drastically. The elements conspired against him again when the drought of the summer of 1787 gave way to the chilly winter of 1787–88. All the while Washington's expenses ballooned from entertaining guests and renovating Mount Vernon's buildings. In a painful comedown, he had been forced repeatedly to dun delinquent debtors. Short of cash, he suffered the indignity of having to press an indebted widow for money from her husband's estate, a task so ghoulish he felt obliged to apologize: "I beg leave to add that it is from the real want of [money] I make such frequent and pressing applications."[60]

On the eve of the Constitutional Convention, Washington had thrown up his hands in despair, confessing to Lund Washington that he could not balance his books: "My estate for the last 11 years have not been able to make both ends meet . . . I mention this for no other purpose than to show that, however willing, I am not able to pay debts unless I could sell land—which I have publicly advertised, without finding bidders."[61] As the convention proceeded, Washington, at his wit's end, told George Augustine that he knew no more "than the man in the moon where I am to get money to pay my taxes"—a shocking admission for a man universally touted as the first president.[62] The failure of his corn crop obligated him to buy eight hundred barrels of corn to feed his army of slaves. Preoccupied with money, Washington hoped the ratification of the Constitution would reverse the country's real estate deflation and alleviate his plight. The day before the Constitution was signed, Washington notified his land agent in western Pennsylvania that he now expected higher prices for his property: "I cannot consent to take two dollars an acre for the land in Washington County. If the government of this country gets well toned and property perfectly secured, I have no doubt of obtaining the price I have fixed on the land, and that in a short time."[63] This turned out to be wishful thinking. Forced to eliminate debt by selling land, he put up for sale a staggering 32,373 acres in the Ohio Country.

As the ratifying conventions progressed, Washington felt a direct financial stake in their outcome, hoping the Constitution would restore American credit. He told one business colleague that the loss of his corn crop and his inability to recoup money from debtors had "caused more perplexity and given me more uneasiness than I ever experienced before from the want of money."[64] Trapped in this predicament, he looked for salvation to the government paper he owned. These promissory notes, used to finance the Revolution, had shed most of their value because of collapsing confidence in the Confederation Congress. Washington had kept these notes, he said, "without having an idea that they would depreciate as they were drawn for interest . . . The injustice of this measure is too obvious and too glaring to pass unobserved."[65] Washington understood firsthand the need for Alexander Hamilton's fiscal program as treasury secretary.

In the spring of 1788 Washington's contemporaries would have been shocked to know that his western taxes for 1785, 1786, and 1787 stood in arrears and that he had posted his lands there for sale to pay them off. Hardly wishing to be a scofflaw at this juncture, Washington tried to pay his taxes promptly with tobacco notes and IOUs that he had received early in the Revolution for supplying articles to the Fairfax County militia. When he learned that Greenbrier County, where the property was located, would not accept such forms of payment, he was enraged. The Father of His Country was being treated with barefaced contempt for financial stresses arising from his wartime sacrifice. "I have been called upon for taxes and threatened at the same time with a sale of the land after June, if the money is not paid before, by the sheriff of Greenbrier County," he wrote. "As I have been suffering loss after loss for near[ly] ten years, while I was in the public service and have scarcely had time to breathe since . . . this procedure seems to me to be a little hasty."[66] In another sign of his eroding financial position, on three occasions he rebuffed the sheriff of Fairfax County when he came around to collect taxes due on Mount Vernon.

By June Washington had paid his outstanding taxes but still seemed cursed by biblical extremes of weather that descended on him with unnerving regularity. "The rains have been so frequent and abundant on *my* plantations that I am, in a manner, drowned," he complained to David Stuart. "What will become of *my* corn is not easy, at this moment to decide. I am working it ankle deep in water and mud."[67] All of Washington's hopes of becoming a model scientific farmer had been scuttled by bad weather.

As Virginia and New York ratified the Constitution during the summer of 1788, Washington's plight had only worsened. That August he told Dr. Craik that "with much truth, I can say I never felt the want of money so sensibly since I was a boy of 15 years old, as I have done for the last 12 months, and probably shall do for 12 months more to come."[68] In other words, Washington foresaw that, if he served as president, he would assume the job amid a full-blown financial crisis. The subsequent year must have been a strange interlude: his name was being bandied about for president as he struggled desperately with his debt load. The day after Christmas 1788 he informed his business agent that "I have never before felt the want of cash so severely as at present."[69] Finally, in early March 1789, after the Electoral College unanimously chose him as president, he took an unprecedented step to salvage his finances. He had suffered a treble blow: another year of poor crops, a continuing inability to collect debts except through long, tedious lawsuits, and the failure to sell land at decent prices. At this nadir of his business life, he sought a loan from a Captain Richard Conway of Alexandria. As he told Conway, "I am inclined to do what I never expected to be reduced to the necessity of doing—that is, to borrow money upon interest. Five hundred pounds would enable me to discharge what I owe in Alexandria . . . and to leave the state (if it shall not be permitted me to remain at home in retirement) without doing this, would be exceedingly disagreeable to me."[70]

No sooner had Washington received the five hundred pounds from Conway at 6 percent interest than he had to request another hundred pounds two days later for "the expenses of my journey to New York, if I go thither."[71] It was an extraordinary admission: Washington needed money to attend his own inauguration as president. Even though he was shortly to receive a presidential salary, he would have to defray the expenses of the executive mansion, imposing yet another gargantuan tax upon his shrinking wealth. One can only imagine Washington's humiliation in cadging money on the eve of his presidency. It would have been especially tough on the tender pride of a man who liked to emit an air of comfortable prosperity. That his second request for money apparently failed could only have aggravated matters.

On March 31, 1789, Washington drew up instructions for George Augustine Washington to guide his supervision of Mount Vernon in his absence. Washington had implicit faith in his nephew's integrity and entrusted him with a general power of attorney. For the next eight years, however distracted he was by his country's affairs, Washington would demand weekly reports down to the minute particulars of wind and weather, and he would send long weekly responses.

Washington's money anxiety had often expressed itself in a sharp tone toward subordinates at Mount Vernon. His financial troubles now added to his recurring frustration with personnel. As his funds dwindled in 1785, he had turned his wrath against his miller. "My miller (William Roberts) is now become such an intolerable sot, and when drunk so great a madman," he complained, "that, however unwilling I am to part with an old servant (for he has been with me 15 years) I cannot with propriety or common justice to myself bear with him any longer."[72] With little confidence in his employees and a deeply rooted reluctance to delegate authority, Washington could not have relished the thought of being absent from Mount Vernon again during his presidency.

A scalding letter that he wrote to his head carpenter, Thomas Green, on March 31, 1789—little more than two weeks before his departure for his inauguration—shows how insecure he felt about leaving his money-losing estate. Always on guard against alcohol abuse, which he branded "the ruin of half the workmen in this country," Washington was exasperated by Green's intractable drinking problem. He warned him that if George Augustine found him unfaithful to his engagements, "either from the love of liquor [or] from a disposition to be running about—or from proneness to idle[ness] when at your work," his nephew had full power "to discard you immediately and to remove your family from their present abode."[73] Not content to leave it at that, Washington grew hotter under the collar, reminding Green that drinking left "a body debilitated, renders him unfit . . . from the execution of [work]. An aching head and trembling limbs, which are the inevitable effects of drinking, disincline the hands from work. Hence begins sloth and that listlessness, which end in idleness." Washington warned him sternly that for the same wages he paid him, he could hire "the best workmen in this country."[74] It was a curiously graceless letter for a man about to ascend to the highest office in the land. Clearly George Washington worried dreadfully about money and whether Mount Vernon would lapse back into the dilapidated state he had found it in more than five years earlier. Now he also had to wonder whether his depleted wealth would support the enhanced celebrity he was about to enjoy as first president of the United States.

PART FIVE

The President

President George Washington,
painted by Gilbert Stuart, 1795–1796.

CHAPTER FORTY-SIX

The Place of Execution

THE CONGRESSIONAL DELAY in certifying Washington's election as president only allowed more time for doubts to fester as he faced the herculean task ahead. He savored his wait as a welcome "reprieve," he told Henry Knox, adding that his "movements to the chair of government will be accompanied with feelings not unlike those of a culprit who is going to the place of his execution."[1] His "peaceful abode" at Mount Vernon, his fears that he lacked the requisite skills for the presidency, the "ocean of difficulties" facing the country—all gave him pause on the eve of his historic journey to New York.[2] In a letter to Edward Rutledge, he made it seem as if the presidency were little short of a death sentence and that, in accepting it, he had given up "all expectations of private happiness in this world."[3] In many ways, the presidency had already come to Mount Vernon as Washington was besieged by obsequious letters from office seekers. "Scarcely a day passes in which applications of one kind or another do not arrive," he told a correspondent.[4] To simplify his life and set a high standard for future presidents, Washington refused to favor friends or relations in making appointments.

The day after Congress counted the electoral votes, declaring Washington the first president, it dispatched Charles Thomson, the secretary of Congress, to bear the official announcement to Mount Vernon. The legislators had chosen a fine emissary. A well-rounded figure, known for his work in astronomy and mathematics, the Irish-born Thomson was a tall, austere man of inborn dignity with a narrow face and keenly penetrating eyes. He couldn't have relished the trip to Virginia, which was "much impeded by tempestuous weather, bad roads, and the many large rivers I had to cross."[5] Yet he rejoiced that the new president would be Washington, whom he revered as singled out by providence to be "the savior and father" of the country.[6] Having known Thomson since the Continental Congress, Washington esteemed him as a faithful public servant and exemplary patriot.

Around noon on April 14, 1789, Washington flung open the door at Mount Vernon and greeted his visitor with a cordial embrace. Once in the privacy of the mansion, he and Thomson conducted a stiff verbal minuet, each man reading from a prepared text. Thomson began by declaring, "I am honored with the commands of the Senate to wait upon your Excellency with the information of your being elected to the office of the President of the United States of America" by a unanimous vote.[7] He read aloud a letter from Senator John Langdon of New Hampshire, the president pro tempore: "Suffer me, sir, to indulge the hope that so auspicious a mark of public confidence will meet your approbation and be considered as a sure sign of the affection and support you are to expect from a free and enlightened people."[8] There was something deferential, even slightly servile, in Langdon's tone, as if he feared that Washington might renege on his pledge and refuse to take the job. Thus was greatness once again thrust upon George Washington.

Any student of Washington's life might have predicted that he would acknowledge his election in a short, self-effacing speech, loaded with disclaimers. "While I realize the arduous nature of the task which is conferred on me and feel my inability to perform it," he replied to Thomson, "I wish there may not be reason for regretting the choice. All I can promise is only that which can be accomplished by an honest zeal."[9] This sentiment of modesty jibed so perfectly with Washington's private letters that it could not have been feigned: he wondered whether he was fit for the post, so unlike anything he had ever done. The hopes for republican government, he knew, rested in his hands. As commander in chief, he been able to wrap himself in a self-protective silence, but the presidency would leave him with no place to hide and would expose him to public censure as nothing before.

Because the vote counting had been long delayed, Washington felt the crush of upcoming public business and decided to set out promptly for New York on April 16, accompanied in his elegant carriage by Thomson and David Humphreys. His diary entry conveys a sense of foreboding: "About ten o'clock, I bade adieu to Mount Vernon, to private life, and to domestic felicity and, with a mind oppressed with more anxious and painful sensations than I have words to express, set out for New York . . . with the best dispositions to render service to my country in obedience to its call, but with less hope of answering its expectations."[10] He sounded like someone marching off, head bowed, to the gallows. Waving goodbye was Martha, who wouldn't join him until mid-May. She watched her husband of thirty years depart with a mixture of bittersweet sensations, wondering "when or whether he will ever come home again." She had long doubted the wisdom of this final act in his public life. "I think it was much too late for him to go into public life again," she told her nephew, "but it was not to be avoided. Our family will be deranged as I must soon follow him."[11]

Determined to travel rapidly, Washington and his entourage set out each day at sunrise and put in a full day on the road. Along the way he hoped to keep ceremonial distractions to a minimum, but he was soon disabused: eight exhausting days of festivities lay ahead. He had traveled only ten miles north to Alexandria when the townspeople waylaid him with a dinner, lengthened by the mandatory thirteen toasts. Adept at farewells, Washington was succinctly eloquent in response: "Unutterable sensations must then be left to more expressive silence, while, from an aching heart, I bid you all, my affectionate friends and kind neighbors, farewell."[12]

Before long, Washington saw that his journey would form the republican equivalent of the procession to a royal coronation. As if already a seasoned politician, he left a trail of political promises in his wake. While in Wilmington, he addressed the Delaware Society for Promoting Domestic Manufacturers and imparted a hopeful message: "The promotion of domestic manufactures will, in my conception, be among the first consequences which may naturally be expected to flow from an energetic government."[13] Arriving in Philadelphia, he was met by local dignitaries and asked to mount a white horse for his entry into town. When he crossed a bridge over the Schuylkill, it was wreathed with laurels and evergreens; at one point a cherubic boy, lowered above him by a mechanical device, popped a laurel crown onto his head. Recurrent cries of "Long Live George Washington" confirmed what James McHenry had already told him before he left Mount Vernon: "You are now a king under a different name."[14]

As Washington entered Philadelphia, he found himself, willy-nilly, at the head of a full-scale parade. Twenty thousand people lined the streets, their eyes fixed on him in wonder. "His Excellency rode in front of the procession, on horseback, politely bowing to the spectators who filled the doors and windows by which he passed," reported the *Federal Gazette,* noting that church bells rang as Washington proceeded to his old haunt, the City Tavern.[15] After the bare-knuckled fight over the Constitution, the newspaper editorialized, Washington had brought the country together: "What a pleasing reflection to every patriotic mind, thus to see our citizens again united in their reliance on this great man who is, a second time, called upon to be the savior of his country!"[16] By the next morning Washington had grown tired of the jubilation. When the light horse cavalry showed up to accompany him to Trenton, they discovered he had sneaked out of the city an hour earlier "to avoid even the appearance of pomp or vain parade," reported one newspaper.[17]

As Washington approached the bridge over Assunpink Creek in Trenton, the spot where he had stood off the British and Hessians, he saw that the townsfolk had erected a magnificent floral arch in his honor with the words "December 26, 1776" sewn from leaves and flowers. Another flowery sentence proclaimed, "The Defenders of the Mothers will also Defend the Daughters."[18] As he rode closer, thirteen young girls, robed in spotless white, walked forward with flower-filled baskets, scattering petals at his feet. Astride his horse, tears standing in his eyes, he returned a deep bow and noted the "astonishing contrast between his former and actual situation at the same spot," declaring he would never forget the present occasion.[19] With that, three rows of women—young girls, unmarried ladies, and married ones—burst into a fervent ode on how he had saved fair virgins and matrons alike. Beneath his public composure, the adulation only crystallized Washington's self-doubt. "I greatly apprehend that my countrymen will expect too much from me," he wrote to Rutledge. "I fear, if the issue of public measures should not correspond with their sanguine expectations, they will turn the extravagant . . . praises which they are heaping upon me at this moment into equally extravagant . . . censures."[20] There was no way, it seemed, that he could lower expectations or escape public reverence.

As Washington approached New York City, a parallel journey from Mount Vernon was in progress that, in many ways, was no less fascinating. Billy Lee, the slave and manservant with whom he had shared so many exploits, longed to join Washington for the inauguration. Once a physical specimen perhaps as imposing as his master, Lee had by now fractured both knees, but he still wanted to make the journey and serve in the presidential household, where he would have to climb three flights of stairs. Dubious that Lee could do it, Washington tried to dissuade him from coming. Nevertheless he always found it difficult to resist Lee's pleas and finally consented that he should travel to the inauguration with Tobias Lear.

When Lear and Lee reached Philadelphia around April 19, Lee's inflamed knees made it impossible for him to soldier on. Lear contacted Clement Biddle and asked if he could minister to Lee until the slave was ready to complete his journey. "Will appears to be in too bad a state to travel at present," Lear wrote. "I shall therefore leave him and will be much obliged to you if you will send him on to New York as soon as he can bear the journey without injury, which I expect will be in two or three days. I shall pay his expenses . . . He dresses his knee himself and therefore will stand in no need of a doctor, unless it should grow worse."[21] In a remarkable act of faith in Lee's fidelity as a slave, Lear left him in Philadelphia while he proceeded to New York. For more than a month, Biddle gave Lee excellent care, calling in two doctors to treat his knee. He even had a steel brace manufactured at "heavy expense" that enabled him to walk, though with difficulty.[22] The care lavished on Billy Lee again confirms that Washington treated him in a singular way among his slaves and dealt with him as a man whose pride and feelings had to be taken into account. From his behavior, it is clear that Washington felt the need to reason with Lee, as if he were an employee, instead of simply bossing him about as a slave. Of course, Lee's exceptional treatment only pointed up the powerless state of other slaves.

Although Lee missed the inauguration, he still yearned for a job in the presidential household. A few days after Washington was inaugurated, Lear wrote to Biddle and tried again to discourage Lee from coming to New York, pointing out that "he cannot possibly be of any service here" and expressing the hope that he would catch the "first vessel that sails for Alex[andri]a" after he recuperated.[23] Lee remained obdurate. Submitting to the slave's wish, Lear instructed Biddle that, if Lee was "still anxious to come on here, the president would gratify him, altho[ugh] he will be troublesome. He has been an old and faithful serv[an]t. This is enough for the president to gratify him in every reasonable wish."[24] On June 22 Lear informed Biddle that "Billy arrived here safe and well."[25] Again, Lear spared no expense with Lee, who was brought by coach from the ferry stop to the presidential mansion. To dress him up for his new duties, Lear went out and got him suitable stockings. Unwilling to spurn Lee's demand for a place in the executive residence, Washington allowed him to work there, probably as a butler, during his first term, even though Lee had, by some accounts, become difficult and temperamental.

By now sated with adulation, Washington preserved a faint hope that he would be allowed to make an inconspicuous entry into New York and pleaded with Governor George Clinton to spare him further hoopla: "I can assure you, with the utmost sincerity, that no reception can be so congenial to my feelings as a quiet entry devoid of ceremony."[26] But he was fooling himself if he imagined he might slip unobtrusively into the temporary capital. Never reconciled to the demands of his celebrity, Washington still fantasized that he could shuck that inescapable burden. When he arrived at Elizabethtown on April 23, an impressive phalanx of three senators, five congressmen, and three state officials awaited him. He must have intuited, with a sinking sensation, that this welcome would eclipse even the frenzied receptions in Philadelphia and Trenton. Moored to the wharf was a special presidential barge, glistening with fresh paint, constructed in his honor and equipped with an awning of red curtains in the rear to shelter him from the elements. To nobody's surprise, the craft was steered by thirteen oarsmen in spanking white uniforms.

As the barge drifted into the Hudson River, Washington made out a Manhattan shoreline already "crowded with a vast concourse of citizens, waiting with exulting anxiety his arrival," a local newspaper said.[27] Many ships anchored in the harbor were garlanded with flags and banners. If Washington gazed back at the receding Jersey shore, he would have seen that his craft led a huge flotilla of boats, including one bearing the portly figure of Henry Knox. Some boats carried musicians and female vocalists on deck, serenading Washington across the waters. "The voices of the ladies were superior to the flutes that played with the stroke of the oars in Cleopatra's silken-corded barge," was the imaginative verdict of the *New York Packet*.[28] These wafted melodies, enhanced by repeated cannon roar and thunderous acclaim from crowds onshore, again oppressed Washington with their implicit message of high expectations. As he confided to his diary, the intermingled sounds "filled my mind with sensations as painful (considering the reverse of this scene, which may be the case after all my labors to do good) as they are pleasing."[29] To guard himself against later disappointment, he seemed not to allow himself the smallest iota of pleasure.

When the presidential barge landed at the foot of Wall Street, Governor Clinton, Mayor James Duane, James Madison, and other luminaries welcomed him to the city. The officer of a special military escort stepped forward briskly and told Washington that he awaited his orders. Washington again labored to cool the celebratory mood. "As to the present arrangement," he replied, "I shall proceed as is directed. But after this is over, I hope you will give yourself no further trouble, as the affection of my fellow-citizens is all the guard I want."[30] Nobody seemed to take the hint seriously.

The streets were solidly thronged with well-wishers, and it took Washington a full hour to arrive at his new residence at 3 Cherry Street, tucked away in the northeastern corner of the city, a block from the East River, near the present-day Brooklyn Bridge. One week earlier the building's owner, Samuel Osgood, had agreed to lease it to Congress as the temporary presidential residence. The descriptions of Washington's demeanor en route to the house confirm that he finally surrendered to the general high spirits, especially when he viewed the legions of adoring women. As Elias Boudinot told his wife, Washington "frequently bowed to the multitude and took off his hat to the ladies at the windows, who waved their handkerchiefs and threw flowers before him and shed tears of joy and congratulation. The whole city was one scene of triumphal rejoicing."[31]

America's second-largest city, with a population of about thirty thousand, New York was a small, provincial town compared to European capitals. Lavishly appointed carriages sped through streets heaped with horse droppings and rubbish. Rich and robust, New York already had a raucous commercial spirit that grated on squeamish sensibilities. "New York is less citified than Philadelphia," said a French visitor, "but the bustle of trade is far greater."[32] Before the war John Adams, passing through town, huffed that "with all the opulence and splendor of this city, there is very little good breeding to be found. There is no modesty. No attention to one another. They talk very loud, very fast, and all together."[33] Although Vice President Adams had arrived before Washington, the town did not endear itself to him on this trip either. Congress had failed to locate a residence for the new vice president, who lodged with John Jay for several weeks.

New York had not yet recovered fully from the dislocations of the war. First Americans and then Britons had uprooted trees and fences for firewood, leaving weed-strewn lots in their path. In the aftermath of the British occupation, said Mayor Duane, New York resembled a place that "had been inhabited by savages or wild beasts."[34] The great conflagration that consumed a quarter of the city in 1776 had left behind blocks of rubble and skeletal houses, some of them yet to be razed. Like many ports, New York catered to a rough, brawling population of sailors and traders and boasted more than four hundred taverns. One French visitor in the 1790s expressed surprise that the city had "whole sections given over to streetwalkers for the plying of their profession" and that it was filled with "houses of debauchery."[35] With its wealthy merchants and brawny laborers, the city already presented a picture of vivid extremes.

Though the Constitution said nothing about an inaugural address, Washington, in an innovative spirit, contemplated such a speech as early as January 1789 and asked a "gentleman under his roof"—David Humphreys—to draft one.[36] Washington had always been economical with words, but the collaboration with Humphreys produced a wordy document, seventy-three pages long, which survives only in tantalizing snippets. In this curious speech, Washington spent a ridiculous amount of time defending his decision to become president, as if he stood accused of some heinous crime. He denied that he had accepted the presidency to enrich himself, even though nobody had accused him of greed: "In the first place, if I have formerly served the community without a wish for pecuniary compensation, it can hardly be suspected that I am at present influenced by avaricious schemes."[37] Addressing a topical concern, he disavowed any desire to found a dynasty, pleading his childless state. Closer in tone to future inaugural speeches was his ringing expression of faith in the American people. He devised a perfect formulation of popular sovereignty, writing that the Constitution had brought forth "a government of the people: that is to say, a government in which all power is derived from, and at stated periods reverts to, them—and that, in its operation . . . is purely a government of laws made and executed by the fair substitutes of the people alone."[38] Showing an Enlightenment spirit, he generalized the American Revolution into a movement blazing a path toward the universal triumph of freedom: "I rejoice in a belief that intellectual light will spring up in the dark corners of the earth; that freedom of inquiry will produce liberality of conduct; that mankind will reverse the absurd position that *the many* were made for *the few;* and that they will not continue slaves in one part of the globe, when they can become freemen in another."[39]

This ponderous speech never saw the light of day. Washington sent a copy to James Madison, who wisely vetoed it on two counts: it was much too long, and its lengthy legislative proposals would be interpreted as executive meddling with the legislature. Instead, Madison drafted for Washington a far more compact speech that avoided tortured introspection. A whirlwind of energy, Madison would seem omnipresent in the early days of Washington's administration. He drafted not only the inaugural address but also the official response by Congress and then Washington's response to Congress, completing the circle. This service established Madison, despite his major role in the House, as a preeminent adviser and confidant to the new president. Oddly enough, he was not troubled that his advisory relationship to Washington might be construed as violating the separation of powers.

Washington knew that everything he did at the swearing-in would establish a tone for the future. "As the first of everything in *our situation* will serve to establish a precedent," he reminded Madison, "it is devoutly wished on my part that these precedents may be fixed on true principles."[40] He would shape indelibly the institution of the presidency. Although he had earned his reputation in battle, he made a critical decision not to wear a uniform at the inauguration or beyond, banishing fears of a military coup. Instead, he would stand there aglitter with patriotic symbols. To spur American manufactures, he would wear a double-breasted brown suit made from broadcloth woven at the Woolen Manufactory of Hartford, Connecticut.[41] The suit had gilt buttons with an eagle insignia on them; to complete his outfit, he would wear white hosiery, silver shoe buckles, and yellow gloves. Washington already sensed that Americans would emulate their presidents. "I hope it will not be a great while before it will be unfashionable for a gentleman to appear in any other dress," he told Lafayette, referring to his American attire. "Indeed, we have already been too long subject to British prejudices."[42] To burnish his image further on inauguration day, Washington powdered his hair and wore a dress sword on his hip, sheathed in a steel scabbard.

The inauguration took place at the building at Wall and Nassau streets that had long served as New York's City Hall. It came richly laden with historical associations, having hosted John Peter Zenger's trial in 1735, the Stamp Act Congress of 1765, and the Confederation Congress from 1785 to 1788. Starting in September 1788, the French engineer Pierre-Charles L'Enfant had remodeled it into Federal Hall, a suitable home for Congress. L'Enfant introduced a covered arcade at street level and a balcony surmounted by a triangular pediment on the second story. As the people's chamber, the House of Representatives was accessible to the public, situated in a high-ceilinged octagonal room on the ground floor, while the Senate met in a second-floor room, buffering it from popular pressure. From this room Washington would emerge onto the balcony to take the oath of office. In many ways, the first inauguration was a hasty, slapdash affair. As with all theatrical spectacles, rushed preparations and frantic work on the new building continued until a few days before the event. Nervous anticipation spread through the city as to whether the two hundred workmen would complete the project on time. Only a few days before the inauguration, an eagle was hoisted onto the pediment, completing the building. The final effect was stately: a white building with a blue and white cupola topped by a weathervane.

A little after noon on April 30, 1789, following a morning filled with clanging church bells and prayers, a contingent of troops on horseback, accompanied by carriages loaded with legislators, stopped at Washington's Cherry Street residence. Escorted by David Humphreys and Tobias Lear, the president-elect stepped into his carriage, which was trailed by foreign dignitaries and crowds of joyous citizens. The procession wound slowly through the narrow Manhattan streets, emerging two hundred yards from Federal Hall. After alighting from his carriage, Washington strode through a double line of soldiers to the building and mounted to the Senate chamber, where members of Congress awaited him expectantly. As he entered, Washington bowed to both houses of the legislature—his invariable mark of respect—then occupied an imposing chair up front. A profound hush settled on the room. Vice President Adams rose for an official greeting, then informed Washington that the epochal moment had arrived: "Sir, the Senate and House of Representatives are ready to attend you to take the oath required by the constitution." "I am ready to proceed," Washington replied.[43]

As he stepped through the door onto the balcony, a spontaneous roar surged from the multitude tightly squeezed into Wall and Broad streets and covering every roof in sight. This open-air ceremony would confirm the sovereignty of the citizens gathered below. Washington's demeanor was stately, modest, and deeply affecting: he clapped one hand to his heart and bowed several times to the crowd. Surveying the serried ranks of people, one observer said they were jammed so closely together that "it seemed one might literally walk on the heads of the people."[44] Thanks to his simple dignity, integrity, and unrivaled sacrifices for his country, Washington's conquest of the people was complete. A member of the crowd, the Count de Moustier, the French minister, noted the solemn trust between Washington and the citizens who stood packed below him with uplifted faces. As he reported to his government, never had "sovereign reigned more completely in the hearts of his subjects than did Washington in those of his fellow citizens . . . He has the soul, look, and figure of a hero united in him."[45] One young woman in the crowd echoed this when she remarked, "I never saw a human being that looked so great and noble as he does."[46] Only Congressman Fisher Ames of Massachusetts noted that "time has made havoc" upon Washington's face, which already looked haggard and careworn.[47]

The sole constitutional requirement for the swearing-in was that the president take the oath of office. That morning a congressional committee decided to add solemnity by having Washington place his hand on a Bible during the oath, leading to a frantic, last-minute scramble to find one. A Masonic lodge came to the rescue by providing a thick Bible, bound in deep brown leather and set on a crimson velvet cushion. By the time Washington appeared on the portico, the Bible rested on a table draped in red velvet.

The crowd grew silent as New York chancellor Robert R. Livingston administered the oath to Washington, who was visibly moved. As he finished the oath, he bent forward, seized the Bible, and brought it to his lips. Washington felt this moment from the bottom of his soul: one observer noted the "devout fervency" with which he "took the oath and the reverential manner in which he bowed down and kissed the Bible."[48] Legend has it that he added "So help me God," though this line was first reported sixty-five years later. Whether or not Washington actually said it, very few people would have heard him anyway, since his voice was soft and breathy. For the crowd below, the oath of office was enacted as a kind of dumbshow. Livingston had to lift his voice and inform the crowd, "It is done." He then intoned: "Long Live George Washington, President of the United States."[49] The spectators responded with huzzas and chants of "God bless our Washington! Long live our beloved President!"[50] They celebrated in the only way they knew, as if greeting a new monarch with the customary cry of "Long Live the King!"

When the balcony ceremony was concluded, Washington returned to the Senate chamber to deliver his inaugural address. In an important piece of symbolism, Congress rose as he entered, then sat down after Washington bowed in response. In England, the House of Commons stood during the king's speeches, so that the seated Congress immediately established a sturdy equality between the legislative and executive branches.

As Washington began his speech, he seemed flustered and thrust his left hand into his pocket while turning the pages with a trembling right hand. His weak voice was barely audible. Fisher Ames evoked him thus: "His aspect grave, almost to sadness; his modesty, actually shaking; his voice deep, a little tremulous, and so low as to call for close attention."[51] Those present attributed Washington's low voice and fumbling hands to anxiety. "This great man was agitated and embarrassed more than ever he was by the leveled cannon or pointed musket," said Senator William Maclay in sniggering tones. "He trembled and several times could scarce make out to read, though it must be supposed he had often read it before."[52] Washington's agitation might have arisen from a developing neurological disorder or might simply have been a bad case of nerves. The new president had long been famous for his physical grace, but the sole gesture he used for emphasis in his speech seemed clumsy—"a flourish with his right hand," said Maclay, "which left rather an ungainly impression."[53] For the next few years Maclay would be a close, unsparing observer of the new president's quirks and tics.

In the first line of his inaugural address, Washington expressed anxiety about his fitness for the presidency, saying that "no event could have filled me with greater anxieties" than the news brought to him by Charles Thomson.[54] He had grown despondent, he said candidly, as he considered his own "inferior endowments from nature" and his lack of practice in civil government.[55] He drew comfort, however, from the fact that the "Almighty Being" had overseen America's birth: "No people can be bound to acknowledge and adore the invisible hand, which conducts the affairs of men, more than the people of the United States."[56] Perhaps referring obliquely to the fact that he suddenly seemed older, he called Mount Vernon "a retreat which was rendered every day more necessary, as well as more dear to me, by the addition of habit to inclination and of frequent interruptions in my health to the gradual waste committed on it by time."[57] In the earlier inaugural address drafted with David Humphreys, Washington had included a disclaimer about his health, telling how he had "prematurely grown old in the service of my country."[58]

Setting the pattern for future inaugural speeches, Washington did not delve into minute policy matters but outlined the big themes that would govern his administration, the foremost being the triumph of national unity over "local prejudices or attachments" that might subvert the country or even tear it apart.[59] National policy needed to be rooted in private morality, which relied on the "eternal rules of order and right" ordained by heaven itself.[60] On the other hand, Washington refrained from endorsing any particular form of religion. Knowing how much was riding on this attempt at republican government, he said that "the sacred fire of liberty, and the destiny of the republican model of government, are justly considered as *deeply,* perhaps as *finally* staked, on the experiment entrusted to the hands of the American people."[61]

After this speech, Washington led a broad procession of delegates up Broadway, along streets flanked by armed militia, to an Episcopal prayer service at St. Paul's Chapel, where he was given his own canopied pew. After these devotions ended, Washington had his first chance to relax until the evening festivities. That night lower Manhattan was converted into a shimmering fairyland of lights. From the residences of Chancellor Livingston and General Knox, Washington observed the fireworks at Bowling Green, a pyrotechnic display that flashed in the sky for two hours. Washington's image was displayed in transparencies hung in many windows, throwing glowing images into the night. Such a celebration, ironically, would have been familiar to Washington from the days when new royal governors arrived in Williamsburg and were greeted by bonfires, fireworks, and illuminations in every window.

All of New York was astir with the evening festivities, and Washington had trouble returning to Cherry Street with Tobias Lear and David Humphreys. "We returned home at ten on foot," wrote Lear, "the throng of people being so great as not to permit a carriage to pass through it."[62] The comment shows how closely people pressed against Washington in the thickly peopled streets. By the time he went to bed, he had initiated many enduring customs for presidential inaugurations, including the procession to the swearing-in venue, taking the oath of office *en plein air*, delivering an inaugural speech, and holding a gigantic celebration that evening. Because Martha was still absent, the inaugural ball was deferred until May.

The odyssey of George Washington from insecure young colonel in the French and Indian War, through his tenure as commander in chief of the Continental Army, and now to president of the new government, must have seemed an almost dream-like progression to him. Perhaps nothing underlined this improbable turn of events more than the extraordinary fact that while Washington had debated whether to become president that winter, on the other side of the ocean King George III had descended into madness. In late January Samuel Powel conveyed this startling piece of news to Washington: "I do not recollect any topic which, at present, occupies the conversation of men so much as the insanity of the king of Great Britain. I am told . . . that Dr. Franklin's observation upon hearing the report was that he had long been of opinion that the King of Great Britain was insane, tho[ugh] it had not been declared to the world till now."[63]

There was nothing vindictive in Washington's nature, no itching for retribution, and he reacted with sympathy to news of the king's malady. "Be the cause of the British king's insanity what it may," he told Powel, "his situation . . . merits commiseration."[64] The strangely contrasting fates of the two Georges grew stranger still in late February, when Gouverneur Morris reported from Paris an unlikely development in the king's madness. "By the bye," he wrote to Washington, "in the melancholy situation to which the poor King of England has been reduced, there were, I am told, in relation to you, some whimsical circumstances." In a deranged fit, wrote Morris, the king had "conceived himself to be no less a personage than George Washington at the head of the American Army. This shows that you have done something or other which sticks most terribly in his stomach."[65] The delusion proved fleeting. On April 23, 1789, exactly one week before George Washington was sworn in to cheering crowds, George III recovered so miraculously from his delusional state that a thanksgiving service was conducted at St. Paul's Cathedral in London. It is hypothesized by some that he had suffered from a rare hereditary disorder called porphyria, a condition not properly diagnosed until the twentieth century. Restored to his senses, he had to contemplate the sobering reality that the upstart George Washington, who had once scrounged for advancement in his royal army, now served as president of an independent American republic.

M ARTHA W ASHINGTON WASN ' T THRILLED at being first lady and, like her husband, talked about the presidency as an indescribable calamity that had befallen her. She professed a lack of interest in politics, having told her niece Fanny the previous year that "we have not a single article of news but politic[s], which I do not concern myself about."[66] Whether she was really so blasé about politics, or merely preferred not to express her opinions, is unclear. The tone of her letters grew wistful as she thought about New York. She and her husband had already sacrificed more than eight years to the war, and after so much hardship Mount Vernon had seemed like their long-deserved sanctuary. Now Washington's presidency would likely eliminate any chance for a private final phase of their lives. Martha couldn't have found it easy to be married to a man who was also married to the nation, but she understood his reasoning in becoming president, telling Mercy Otis Warren that she could not blame him "for having acted according to his ideas of duty in obeying the voice of his country."[67]

Martha Washington never defied her husband openly, but when forced to do anything against her will, she could be quietly willful. She would pout and sulk and drag her feet in silence. In one letter Washington said that he wanted to be "well fixed at New York" before he sent for her, but one suspects that Martha's delay reflected her disinclination to leave Virginia.[68] A few days after his inauguration, Washington wrote with some urgency to George Augustine, asking him to hasten Martha's departure, "for we are extremely desirous of seeing her here."[69] This suggests that her delay had lasted longer than expected. By that point, Washington knew that she would miss the ceremonial ball planned for May 7 at the Assembly Rooms on Broadway. Evidently Martha's presence had been anticipated, for a special elevated sofa had been created that would enable the president and first lady to preside in state over the celebration.

On May 14 Washington's nephew, nineteen-year-old Robert Lewis, arrived at Mount Vernon to escort his aunt to New York and discovered with amazement that "everything appeared to be in confusion."[70] Martha was still supervising the packing in an unusually chaotic scene for this well-organized woman. Finally on May 16, with one wagon heaped with nothing but baggage, she piled into her coach with her two grandchildren, Nelly and Washy, accompanied by a retinue of six slaves. As a crowd of slaves clustered around the departing group, emotions ran high. "The servants of the house and a number of the field Negroes made their appearance to take leave of their mistress," Robert Lewis recorded in his journal. "Numbers of these poor wretches seemed greatly *agitated, much affected*. My aunt equally so."[71] The slaves' tears were surely genuine, but one wonders whether they were shed for the six friends and family members being forcibly relocated to New York; perhaps the remaining slaves feared mistreatment at the hands of overseers in the Washingtons' absence. Martha decided to take two personal slaves, Molly (or Moll) and a sixteen-year-old mulatto girl named Ona (or Oney) Judge, who had become her favorite. Two other slaves, Austin and Christopher Sheels, would act as waiters in New York, while Giles and Paris, who had accompanied Washington to the Constitutional Convention, would reprise their roles as coachmen.

The Martha Washington who set out for New York was a more matronly woman than the doughty wife who showed up regularly at the Continental Army camp each winter. Like her husband, she now wore spectacles on occasion. Ever dutiful, she did her best to live up to her new station on the national scene. With political instincts to rival her husband's, she had ordered green and brown wool from Hartford to make riding costumes for herself and was lauded in the press for being "clothed in the manufacture of our country."[72]

En route to New York, Martha had no better luck than her husband in escaping the hordes who competed to greet her. Nevertheless, as she got her first taste of being first lady—the term was not adopted until later administrations—she experienced a rising sense of excitement. Upon reaching the outskirts of Philadelphia, she was hailed by the state's chief executive, and a cavalry honor guard conducted her into town. On May 27 the new president took time out from his duties to receive his wife at Elizabethtown, where she got the same tumultuous reception bestowed on him a month earlier. As Martha wrote appreciatively to Fanny, the welcoming committee had come "with the fine barge you have seen so much said of in the papers, with the same oarsmen that carried the P[resident] to New York."[73] Little Washy Custis was flabbergasted by the boat ride and by the grand parade that swept up the entire party the moment the big, burly governor of New York, George Clinton, received them on the Manhattan side. Meanwhile sister Nelly spent hours at the window on Cherry Street, transfixed by the fancy carriages passing down below.

No sooner had she arrived in the capital than Martha learned that she would be a prop in an elaborate piece of political theater. One day after her arrival, she had to host a dinner for congressional leaders, and the day after that, all of New York society seemed to cram into the Cherry Street mansion for her first reception—a function for which she had not been consulted. She was plunged into a giddy whirl of activity. "I have not had one half hour to myself since the day of my arrival," she told Fanny in early June.[74] She narrated this abrupt transformation with a note of quiet wonder: the woman who had been dubious about this new life sounded positively breathless with amazement. She had been taken in hand by a professional hairdresser, a novel experience for her. "My hair is set and dressed every day and I have put on white muslin habits for the summer," she wrote home in early June. "You would, I fear, think me a good deal in the fashion if you could but see me."[75]

The town was enchanted with Martha Washington, whose conviviality offset her husband's reserve. She won over the toughest critic: the wife of the vice president, who found her the perfect republican counterpart of her husband. "I took the earliest opportunity . . . to go and pay my respects to Mrs. Washington," Abigail Adams informed her sister. "She received me with great ease and politeness. She is plain in her dress, but that plainness is the best of every article . . . Her hair is white, her teeth beautiful, her person rather short than otherwise."[76] The favorable impression grew upon second viewing: "Mrs. Washington is one of those unassuming characters which create love and esteem. A most becoming pleasantness sits upon her countenance and an unaffected deportment which renders her the object of veneration and respect."[77]

A pragmatic woman, Martha Washington resigned herself to the duties of a presidential wife, but a distinct touch of discontent lingered. She was quietly rebellious, chafing at her restricted freedom. In late October she unburdened herself to Fanny: "I live a very dull life here and know nothing that passes in the town. I never go to the public place. Indeed, I think I am more like a state prisoner than anything else." She complained of "certain bounds set for me which I must not depart from. And as I cannot do as I like, I am obstinate and stay at home a great deal."[78] Obviously there were limits to her acquiescence, and she adopted an increasingly satiric tone when talking about the fashionable people of New York. When she sent Fanny a watch, she described it as "of the newest fashion, if that has any influence on your taste." Then she added tartly: "It will last as long as the fashion—and by that time you can get another of a fashionable kind."[79]

At year's end Martha Washington aired her frustrations to Mercy Otis Warren, pointing out that her grandchildren and Virginia family constituted the major source of her happiness: "I shall hardly be able to find any substitute that would indemnify me for the loss of a part of such endearing society."[80] She knew other women would gladly swap places with her: "With respect to myself, I sometimes think the arrangement is not quite as it ought to have been—that I, who had much rather be at home, should occupy a place with which a great many younger and gayer women would be prodigiously pleased."[81] But she would not rail against her destiny: "I am still determined to be cheerful and to be happy in whatever situation I may be, for I have also learned from experience that the greater part of our happiness or misery depends upon our dispositions and not upon our circumstances."[82] To the end of her life, Martha Washington would speak forlornly of the presidential years as her "lost days."[83]

CHAPTER FORTY-SEVEN

Acting the Presidency

WHEN GEORGE WASHINGTON BECAME PRESIDENT, the executive departments had not yet been formed or their chieftains installed, so he placed unusual reliance on his personal secretaries, whom he dubbed "the gentlemen of the household."[1] He put a premium on efficiency, good manners, discretion, and graceful writing. The staff mainstay was Harvard-educated Tobias Lear, the agreeable young man brought up from Mount Vernon. In these early days Lear was a man for all seasons: dashing off private letters for Washington, cranking out dinner invitations, tending files, tutoring grandchildren, accompanying Washington on afternoon strolls or Martha on shopping sprees. So trusted was Lear that he kept the household accounts, and Washington turned to him for petty cash. His loyalty had no limits. "I have never found a single thing that could lessen my respect for him," Lear remarked of Washington. "A complete knowledge of his honesty, uprightness, and candor in all his private transactions has sometimes led me to think him more than a man."[2] When Lear married Polly Long in April 1790—Martha called her "a pretty, sprightly woman"—the Washingtons invited the young couple to share their household, enriching their lives with an extended family as they had done at Mount Vernon.[3]

For a second secretary, Washington retained David Humphreys, with his agile pen. Now seasoned by diplomatic experience in Paris with Jefferson, Humphreys advised Washington on questions of etiquette and was anointed chamberlain, or master of ceremonies, for the administration. The third team member was Major William Jackson, an orphan from South Carolina who had won high marks as secretary of the Constitutional Convention, having taken notes of the deliberations while preserving their secrecy—a man of discretion after Washington's own heart.

The closest that Washington came to a security guard, Jackson remained a protective presence at his side, whether he was out walking, riding, or performing official duties. Rounding out the group were Thomas Nelson, Jr., son of the late Virginia governor, and Washington's young nephew Robert Lewis, who had escorted his aunt Martha to New York.

Among members of Congress, James Madison stood in a class by himself in his advisory capacity to Washington. When he ran for Congress, Madison had consulted Washington about how to campaign without descending to crass electioneering. It is not surprising that Washington leaned on Madison early in his presidency, since nobody possessed a more nuanced grasp of the Constitution. In 1789 Congress had to shape both the executive and the judicial branches, which would act to enhance Madison's prestige. Gradually, as the three branches of government assumed more separate characters and political differences between the two men surfaced, Madison shed his advisory role.

By the time Washington was sworn in, the federal government had already been set in motion; the first order of business was to generate money to guarantee the new government's survival. Three weeks before the inauguration, Madison introduced in the House a schedule of duties on imported goods to provide revenues. Nothing better proclaimed the new government's autonomy: the impotent Confederation Congress had never commanded an independent revenue stream.

Washington's first days in office were dominated by seemingly trivial symbolic issues that spoke to larger questions about the character of the new government. "Many things which appear of little importance in themselves . . . at the beginning may have great and durable consequences, from their having been established at the commencement of a new general government," Washington instructed Vice President Adams.[4] Every action, he knew, would be subjected to exhaustive scrutiny: "My political conduct . . . must be exceedingly circumspect and proof against just criticism, for the eyes of Argus [the hundred-eyed monster in Greek mythology] are upon me and no slip will pass unnoticed."[5] Washington had long felt those searching eyes trained upon him and would try hard as president to be a paragon.

Of the various government posts, it was the presidency that had the potential to slip into monarchy and subvert republican government, so every decision made about it aroused a firestorm of controversy. For many Americans, presidential etiquette seemed like the back door through which aristocratic corruption might infiltrate the system. On April 23 the Senate appointed a committee to devise suitable titles for addressing the president. Vice President Adams favored highfalutin ones. "A royal, or at least a princely, title, will be found indispensably necessary to maintain the reputation, authority, and dignity of the president," he insisted.[6] The final Senate recommendation was absurdly pretentious: "His Highness, the President of the United States of America, and Protector of their Liberties."[7] Sensitive to criticism that high-flown titles were reminiscent of monarchy, Washington gladly accepted the simpler form adopted by the House: "The President of the United States." An approving Madison later noted that Washington had been irritated by efforts to "bedizen him with a superb but spurious title."[8] The controversy served notice on Washington that such matters had powerful resonance as the new republic tried to find dignified forms that didn't smack of European decadence. "Nothing could equal the ferment and disquietude occasioned by the proposition respecting titles," David Stuart wrote from Virginia. "As it is believed to have originated from Mr. Adams and [Richard Henry] Lee, they are not only unpopular to an extreme, but highly odious."[9]

For Washington, the etiquette issue was also related to how he would preserve his privacy and sanity as president. From the time he occupied the Cherry Street mansion, he found himself hounded by legislators, office seekers, veterans, and well-wishers. Before long, he felt himself under siege, unable to accomplish any work. After making inquiries, he learned that presidents of the Confederation Congress had been "considered in no better light than as a maitre d'hotel . . . for their table was considered as a public one."[10] As in everything else, Washington operated in uncharted waters. "I was unable to attend to any business whatsoever," he told Stuart, "for gentlemen, consulting their own convenience rather than mine, were calling from the time I rose from breakfast—often before—until I sat down to dinner."[11] With his days cluttered with ceremonial visits, Washington complained, "I had no leisure to read or answer the dispatches which were pouring in from all quarters."[12] As he tried to barricade himself from strangers, he wondered how he could avoid the extremes of either rebuffing visitors in a "mimickry of royalty" or becoming so secluded that he would shut out important communications. In short, how to find the "discriminating medium"?[13]

As he had always done, Washington solicited written opinions from several advisers, including Adams, Madison, Hamilton, Jay, and Robert R. Livingston, from which he would distill his preferred policy. The hallmark of his administration would be an openness to conflicting ideas. In wartime Washington had urged officers to find a happy medium between being too close to and too remote from their men. Now, in remarkably similar language, he told Madison that he wanted to avoid the "charge of superciliousness" if he held himself too aloof, as well as the diminished presidential dignity that might arise from "too free an intercourse and too much familiarity."[14] In many ways, Washington's solution borrowed from two worlds, adapting kingly traditions to a republican ethos. Presidential conduct would be true to revolutionary principles but imbued with the forms of polite society that Washington had known his entire life.

To strike a proper balance, Hamilton suggested that Washington hold weekly levees—the term was borrowed from royal receptions—in which visitors could chat with him. The president would enter, remain half an hour, make small talk with guests, then disappear. A man of congenital formality, who kept an impenetrable zone of privacy around himself, Washington did not enjoy socializing with strangers, so Hamilton's scenario held an obvious appeal. The latter also suggested dinners with small groups of legislators, especially senators who shared with the president constitutional responsibilities, such as concluding foreign treaties and approving major appointments. "This makes them, in a degree, his constitutional counselors," Hamilton noted.[15] He also recommended that Washington refuse invitations to dine elsewhere, lest it impair presidential authority. Washington sympathized with any proposal that curtailed his social obligations. "I have no relish for formal and ceremonious engagements," he explained to James McHenry, "and only give in to them when they cannot be avoided."[16]

To handle the stampede of people wishing to see him, Washington decided to hold his levees every Tuesday afternoon at three P.M. The newspapers let it be known that, on other days, visits would "not be agreeable" to the president.[17] Guests would need introductions from suitable personages. Ordinarily Washington's secretaries would assist them from their carriages, but the president was capable of performing this courtesy when ladies and old comrades came calling. When the widows of Nathanael Greene and Richard Montgomery appeared, for instance, Washington went outside to help them down from their carriages.

The president was a punctual man, and, precisely at three, the folding doors of his dining room were flung open to guests; at three-fifteen, they were shut to further visitors. By the time guests arrived, Washington had struck a stately pose by the fireplace, encased in rigid protocol. The room was largely empty, most of the furniture having been cleared to make space. Since Washington's hearing was failing, David Humphreys announced him and his visitors in a raised voice. At the first levee Humphreys announced Washington in such a loud, pompous voice that, according to Madison, Washington shot him a reproachful look.

In a well-directed sequence, visitors came in and bowed to Washington, who then bowed in return before they took their place in a standing circle. With an excellent memory for names, Washington seldom required a second introduction. In a manner that reminded some of European kings, Washington never shook hands, holding on to a sword or a hat to avoid direct contact with people. Slowly he made the round of standing visitors, chatting briefly with each, then resuming his original position by the fireplace. Then the guests, moving like so many marionettes, came up to him one by one, bowed, and went their way. The reception concluded promptly at the stroke of four. Like a stage actor leaving nothing to chance, Washington reproduced this ritual exactly each week. Small wonder that John Adams said that if Washington "was not the greatest president, he was the best actor of the presidency we have ever had."[18]

One guest, describing the president's magnificent presence, recalled

> the tall manly figure of Washington clad in black velvet; his hair in full dress, powdered and gathered behind in a large silk bag; yellow gloves on his hands; holding a cocked hat with a cockade in it, and the edges adorned with a black feather about an inch deep. He wore knee and shoe buckles; and a long sword, with a finely wrought and polished steel hilt, which appeared at the left hip; the coat worn over the sword, so that the hilt, and the part below the folds of the coat behind, were in view. The scabbard was white polished leather.[19]

From the description, one can see how meticulously Washington fashioned the image that he broadcast to the world. Walter Buchanan, a New York physician, left a revealing tale of a visit to the Cherry Street mansion during the president's first Fourth of July in office. When told that a small delegation from the Society of the Cincinnati had appeared on his doorstep, Washington disappeared upstairs, donned his black velvet suit and dress sword, then invited the veterans in for cakes and wine. "On their departure," noted Buchanan, "the general again retired and came down to dinner in his usual costume of pepper-and-salt colored clothes."[20]

The Tuesday-afternoon levees, wooden and boring, were excruciating affairs, unrelieved by spontaneity. Washington's heroic stature, an essential part of his strength, was turned into a plaster cast that imprisoned him. During these scripted functions, people found it impossible to engage in substantive discussions with him, and perhaps that was the point. The taciturn Washington could see people without worrying that they would solicit him for jobs or pump him for political opinions. In searching for the happy medium between "much state" and "too great familiarity," Washington largely succeeded in finding it.[21] Despite the benign look in his eye, he managed to preserve a certain official distance. "He is polite with dignity," Abigail Adams attested that spring, "affable without formality, distant without haughtiness, grave without austerity, modest, wise, and good."[22]

Since Washington's Tuesday levees were limited to men, he and Martha decided that she would entertain female visitors every Friday evening from seven to ten, serving tea, coffee, ice cream, and lemonade. The plump little Martha, seated on a sofa as guests entered, enjoyed sampling the desserts. She dressed well but avoided jewelry as inappropriate for the new republic and was addressed by the democratic nomenclature of "Mrs. Washington." Never a sparkling talker, she was invariably a capable one, falling easily into conversation with people and making even complete strangers feel welcome. Usually seated at her right elbow was Abigail Adams, who noted how Washington chided anyone who violated protocol: "The president never fails of seeing that [the seat] is relinquished for me, and having removed ladies several times, they have now learnt to rise and give it to me."[23]

Dispensing with hat and sword, Washington made a minor concession to informality by wearing a brown coat on Friday evenings. More relaxed than at his own levees, he circulated and chatted amiably with guests, displaying "a grace, dignity, and ease that leaves Royal George far behind him," Abigail Adams reported.[24] Washington delighted in the company of pretty women, who found his appeal only heightened by the presidency. "The young ladies used to throng around him and engage him in conversation," said one visitor. "There were some of the well-remembered *belles* of that day, who imagined themselves to be favorites with him. As these were the only opportunities which they had of conversing with him, they were disposed to use them."[25] Another observer noted that Washington seemed less austere at his wife's teas, where he "talks more familiarly with those he knows and sometimes with the ladies."[26] Washington never engaged in flirtatious looks, but he unquestionably paid special attention to women in attendance. "The company this evening was thin, especially of ladies," he complained in his diary after one Friday soirée.[27] Because the Washingtons rose early, Martha often terminated the gatherings before the allotted ten o'clock deadline, saying that she and the president had to go to bed.

Even as the Washingtons sought an optimal balance between presidential splendor and republican austerity, an opposition press emerged that accused them of trying to foist a monarchy on the country. For anyone who had seen the opulence of Versailles or Windsor Castle, such accusations would have seemed wildly overblown. But every revolution breeds fears of counterrevolution, and worries about a reversion to monarchism were perhaps predictable after a war against royal absolutism. Each morning as he read the gazettes, Washington was stung by commentary on his receptions. Berating his dinners, the *Daily Advertiser* warned readers that "in a few years we shall have all the paraphernalia yet wanting to give the superb finish to the grandeur of our AMERICAN COURT! The purity of republican principle seems to be daily losing ground . . . We are on the eve of another revolution."[28] Even Martha's rather wholesome Friday-night gatherings were depicted darkly in some quarters as "court-like levees" and "queenly drawing rooms."[29] When Washington's birthday was celebrated in February 1790 as a national holiday, purists disparaged it as yet another showy monarchical exercise.

Among the leading critics of Washingtonian excess was William Maclay, the caustic senator from Pennsylvania with a thin, bony face. The son of Scotch-Irish Presbyterian immigrants, Maclay had a pronounced populist streak that predisposed him to spot signs of incipient monarchy. In June 1789 he recorded his private fears that fancy people around town had seduced the president: "Indeed, I entertain not a doubt but many people are aiming, with all their force, to establish a splendid court with all the pomp of majesty. Alas, poor Washington, if you are taken in this snare, how will the gold become dim?"[30]

In copious diary entries, written with the satirical eye of a gadfly, Maclay left vivid impressions of President Washington in social situations during his first term. An eager purveyor of gossip, Maclay was scarcely objective, taking a mordant, often jaundiced, view of people. Sometimes his tattle was downright mean-spirited, as when Robert Morris's wife told him of a presidential dinner at which she bit into a dessert only to find it full of rancid cream. When informed of it, the president "changed his plate immediately. But, she added with a titter, Mrs. Washington ate a whole heap of it."[31] His observations could be laced with patent envy: "No Virginian can talk on any subject but the perfections of Gen[era]l Washington."[32]

Nonetheless, Maclay left some priceless glimpses into the social world of George and Martha Washington, whom he satirized as boors and bumpkins, overshadowed by more elegant couples they were trying to impress. He reported Washington's misery in social settings, picking up little fidgety habits that showed him enduring these occasions rather than enjoying them. He did not realize how much Washington hated dealing with so many strangers. In trying to impart dignity to presidential protocol, Washington sometimes became frozen in this studied role, eliminating the levity and conversational flow that enlivened at least some dinners at Mount Vernon or with his military family during the war.

Every other Thursday the Washingtons held an official dinner at four P.M. The president, seeking geographic diversity, often tried to balance northern and southern legislators on his guest list. If guests were even five minutes late by the hall clock, they found the president and his company already seated. Washington would then explain curtly that the cook was governed by the clock and not by the company. In his diary, Maclay described a dinner on August 27, 1789, in which George and Martha Washington sat in the middle of the table, facing each other, while Tobias Lear and Robert Lewis sat on either end. John Adams, John Jay, and George Clinton were among the assembled guests. Maclay described a table bursting with a rich assortment of dishes—roasted fish, boiled meat, bacon, and poultry for the main course, followed by ice cream, jellies, pies, puddings, and melons for dessert. Washington usually downed a pint of beer and two or three glasses of wine, and his demeanor grew livelier once he had consumed them.

Maclay painted a deadly portrait of Washington at one dinner as a veteran bore, devoid of conversation except platitudes, and very jittery: "The president kept a fork in his hand when the cloth was taken away—I thought for the purpose of picking nuts. He ate no nuts, but played with the fork, striking on the edge of the table with it."[33] Washington could neither relax nor converse spontaneously, leading Maclay to conclude that "it was the most solemn dinner ever I ate at . . . The ladies sat a good while and the bottles passed about, but there was a dead silence almost."[34]

On March 4, 1790, Maclay wrote an account of another stifling dinner and again portrayed a consistently somber Washington: "The president seemed to bear in his countenance a settled aspect of melancholy. No cheering ray of convivial sunshine broke thro[ugh] the cloudy gloom of settled seriousness. At every interval of eating or drinking, he played on the table with a fork or knife, like a drumstick."[35] Sitting at Washington's right side, John Adams fared no better at the hands of Maclay, who derided the vice president as "mantling his visage with the most unmeaning simper that ever dimpled the face of folly."[36] Senator Samuel Johnston of North Carolina, who attended the same dinner, was entranced by it: "I have just left the president's, where I had the pleasure of dining with almost every member of the Senate. We had some excellent champagne and after it, I had the honor of drinking coffee with his lady, a most amiable woman. If I live much longer, I believe that I shall at last be reconciled to the company of old women for her sake."[37]

Two months later, finding Washington in better spirits, Maclay provided a possible clue to the awkward silences of earlier gatherings: "Went to dine with the president, agreeable to invitation. He seemed more in good humor than ever I saw him, tho[ugh] he was so deaf that I believe he heard little of the conversation."[38] That Washington's hearing had deteriorated—not surprising after eight years of roaring cannon—may explain the gruesome conversational gaps that Maclay so freely mocked. Deafness can be an isolating experience, especially for a president. People would naturally have waited for him to respond to statements before proceeding with the conversation; to conceal his deafness, a self-conscious Washington may well have feigned hearing what they said and sat there in silence. It was yet another sign of the aging process that had transformed the once dashing, athletic Washington.

On January 20, 1791, Maclay, a lame duck senator, attended a last dinner with the president. Though Maclay had developed into a sharp political opponent, the president still treated him with instinctive decorum, not the royal hauteur of his imaginings. Maclay took a final measure of the man, and his description shows how dramatically time had altered Washington: "Let me take a review of him as he really is. In stature about six feet, with an unexceptionable make, but lax appearance. His frame would seem to want filling up. His motions rather slow than lively, tho[ugh] he showed no signs of having suffered either by gout or rheumatism. His complexion pale, nay, almost cadaverous. His voice hollow and indistinct owing, as I believe, to artificial teeth before in his upper jaw."[39]

Washington had clearly undergone a startling change. Described as "lusty" by Robert Hunter in 1785, he was now slow and shuffling. Instead of being ruddy with buoyant health, he was gaunt and "cadaverous." Where earlier observers had commented on his well-padded muscles, Washington's frame now wanted "filling up." And the voice was again described as thin and whispery. An unaccustomed stiffness had overtaken his movements, he knew. When one Virginian criticized his clumsy bows at receptions, he said they were "the best I was master of" and remarked plaintively to David Stuart, "Would it not have been better to have thrown the veil of charity over them, ascribing their stiffness to the effects of age . . . than to pride and dignity of office, which, God knows, has no charms for me?"[40]

According to Jefferson, Washington told him that "nobody disliked more the ceremonies of his office and he had not the least taste or gratification in the execution of its function; that he was happy at home alone."[41] Suffering from the stultifying etiquette imposed by his office, he later railed against those who had prescribed such formality. He was especially upset that, having tried to strike a balance between pomp and austerity, he had been roundly criticized and misunderstood. As Jefferson wrote after a 1793 conversation, Washington "expressed the extreme wretchedness of his existence while in office and went lengthily into the late attacks on him for levees etc., and explained to me how he had been led into them by the persons he consulted at New York and that, if he could but know what the sense of the public was, he would most cheerfully conform to it."[42]

Washington found it hard to live frugally, and the chief steward he hired to supervise the kitchen made economy that much more difficult. Sam Fraunces had formerly owned the tavern at which Washington had enacted his lachrymose farewell to his officers at the war's end.[43] In the mid-1780s Fraunces had run into serious debt and even appealed to Washington for financial aid. By the time Washington hired him to manage his household, Fraunces had opened another tavern on Cortlandt Street.

A shrewd operator with a flamboyant manner, Fraunces seemed ubiquitous at Washington's dinner parties, "resplendently dressed in wig and small-clothes," according to one historian.[44] A skillful cook, he knew how to dress a table, supervise waiters, prepare desserts, and bring forth a sumptuous meal. Somewhat to Washington's chagrin, Fraunces preened himself on the "bountiful and elegant" dinners he presented.[45] Tobias Lear stared agog at the heaps of lobster, oysters, and other dishes, saying Fraunces "tossed up such a number of fine dishes that we are distracted in our choice when we sit down to table and obliged to hold a long consultation upon the subject, before we can determine what to attack."[46] In time Washington began to reprimand his steward for unconscionable extravagance. However fond he was of lavish living, he minded his pennies and personally reviewed household bills.

Unfortunately, the feisty Fraunces wasn't one to be deterred, not even by a sitting president. "Well he may discharge me," Frances declared. "He may kill me if he will, but while he is President of the United States and I have the honor to be his steward, his establishment shall be supplied with the very best of everything that the whole country can afford."[47] Washington's attempts to rein in Fraunces led to a running battle that raged until Fraunces quit in February 1790. To show there were no hard feelings, Washington bestowed on him a last bonus for his tavern.

Even before Washington occupied 3 Cherry Street, he had grumbled about the cost of renovating it. The handsome three-story building had a high stoop, balusters along the roof, and seven fireplaces inside. It stood on a boisterous thoroughfare crawling with traffic. The day before Washington arrived, Sally Robinson, niece of owner Samuel Osgood, inspected the premises and found "every room furnished in the most elegant manner," she told a friend. "The best of furniture in every room and the greatest quantity of plate and china I ever saw. The whole of the first and second stories [are] papered and the floors covered with the richest kinds of Turkey and Wilton carpets . . . There is scarcely anything talked about now but General Washington and the Palace."[48] For all the fuss made over the house, it did not work well for the Washingtons. It had to house thirty people and was sufficiently cramped that three secretaries—Humphreys, Nelson, and Lewis—slept in a single room on the third floor. Humphreys, then writing a play, reportedly strode the hall after dark in his nightshirt, loudly declaiming verse from the epilogue. The house was located at an inconvenient spot near the East River, distant from the tony seats of government and society situated on Broadway.

The impresario of entertaining, Washington took personal charge of selecting the ornaments that defined the grandeur of his dining room. Far from shunting off decorating on his wife or subordinates, he trusted his detailed knowledge of the decorative arts. To create a tea service, he melted down some old silver and had the finished products engraved with his griffin crest. When he asked Gouverneur Morris, then resident in Europe, to purchase wine coolers for dinners, he showed a characteristic concern with orderly appearance. To keep the wine cool, the bottles would be placed in silver wire baskets partly immersed in ice. Washington issued precise instructions for their manufacture so that "whether full or empty, the bottles will always stand upright and never be at variance with each other." [49] With an educated eye for furnishings that might lend brilliance to state dinners, he also had Morris ship him decorative mirrors for the tabletop, so that silverware and candlesticks would emit shimmering reflections. As if part of his job were refining American taste, Washington oversaw the purchase of many objets d'art, including porcelain figures, silver spoons, and a china set embellished with the eagle of the Society of the Cincinnati.

No small part of the splendor of Washington's establishment was his household contingent of twenty servants, seven of them slaves. All the servants, white and black, were buffed to a high gloss. A few slaves were bedecked in the same costumes as the white servants: a white livery with red trim on the cuffs and collars. Cocked hats, gloves, and well-polished shoes completed the glossy outfit. To posterity, it seems shocking that Washington imported slaves into the presidential mansion, but Jefferson would bring a dozen slaves from Monticello to the White House; the tradition of having slaves in the presidential household unfortunately lasted until the death in 1850 of Zachary Taylor, the last of the slaveholding presidents.

Washington extended the grandeur of his presidency to morning horseback rides. He kept a dozen horses in New York and made a daily a tour of his stables. Aware of how impressive he looked atop a white mount, he once instructed a friend to buy him a horse, specifying that he "would prefer a *perfect* white."[50] In the early days of his presidency, he rode a pair of spotless white parade horses, Prescott and Jackson. Perhaps he had a subliminal memory of Lord Botetourt riding to the palace in colonial Williamsburg behind a coach with shining white horses. So taken was Washington with his unblemished chargers that he had grooms rub them with white paste at night, bundle them in cloths, then bed them down on fresh straw. In the morning the hardened white paste gleamed, its paleness accentuated by black polish applied to the horses' hooves. For command performances, the animals' mouths were rinsed and their teeth scrubbed. In another fancy touch, Washington set his saddles in leopard skins edged with gold braiding.

On a fine spring day New York residents might glimpse the president and first lady out for a ride in their ornate, varnished coach, drawn by six well-matched bay horses. With four postilions attired in leather breeches and glazed leather hats, the coach made an exquisite impression as it rolled through the crowded streets. "When he travels," a British diplomat later observed, "it is in a very kingly style."[51] Sometimes the Washingtons stared out the window and at other times drew the Venetian blinds or black leather curtains for privacy. In 1790 Washington adorned the coach with allegorical scenes of the four seasons, executed on the outside panels, affixing his personal crest to four small quarter panels.

Occasionally in the early afternoon, Washington descended from Mount Olympus and ambled through the city streets, where he greeted citizens in a more egalitarian manner. On one such promenade, he encountered in a shop six-year-old Washington Irving, attended by a Scottish maid. "Please your honor," said the maid, pushing the little boy forward, "here's a bairn [child] was named after you."[52] Washington patted the head of the little boy fated to be his future biographer. That Washington walked the streets and made himself accessible to ordinary people carried important political overtones. As David Stuart reported from Virginia, "It has given me much pleasure to hear every part of your conduct spoke[n] of with high approbation, and particularly your dispensing with ceremony occasionally and walking the streets, while [John] Adams is never seen but in his carriage and six."[53]

Another place Washington encountered New Yorkers was at his presidential pew at St. Paul's Chapel, where he often appeared on Sunday mornings. He devoted Sunday afternoons to writing lengthy communications to George Augustine Washington about Mount Vernon matters, ranging from crop rotation to mule breeding. On Sunday evenings he read aloud sermons or passages from Scriptures and continued to say grace at meals. An integral component of his religiosity was his charitable largesse to the indigent and others in need. When destitute veterans flocked to his door, Washington frequently dispensed alms to them. He gave scores of charitable contributions, preferring anonymity, though he sometimes made exceptions on public holidays to set an example for the citizenry. After he designated Thursday, November 26, 1789, as the first Thanksgiving Day, for example, he contributed beer and food to those jailed for debt.

Washington lost no time becoming a regular visitor to the John Street Theater. A simple red wooden building, large and bare as a barn, it had its own presidential box, emblazoned with the arms of the United States. When the theater manager told Washington that he usually started plays at seven P.M. but would gladly delay them until his arrival, Washington set him straight, saying he would always be punctual and that the audience would never have to wait. Washington invariably appeared at seven on the dot. The instant he did, the orchestra struck up "The President's March," later known as "Hail, Columbia," and the audience erupted with robust cheers. Since Washington's presence was typically announced in advance, the performances usually drew veterans who doffed their caps and waved up to him.

At the time theatergoing was still considered a bit racy. When Washington invited John and Sarah Jay to join him in his box, he said he would understand if they declined from "any reluctance to visiting the theater."[54] The Jays accepted with pleasure. That George Washington was a habitué of risqué plays indicates he was hardly a prude. The first play he saw, on May 11, 1789, was his all-time satirical favorite, William Sheridan's *The School for Scandal*. His box was large enough to accommodate several guests, and he invited along Senator Maclay. Even the curmudgeonly Maclay was thrilled by the experience and regretted not having brought his children: "Long might one of them [have] live[d] to boast of their having been seated in the same box with the first character in the world."[55] That box was often packed with government dignitaries and leading personalities. On the evening of November 24, 1789, the Washingtons were joined by Abigail Adams, Alexander and Elizabeth Hamilton, Philip Schuyler, and Catharine "Caty" Greene, the general's widow. Such evenings constituted a perfect form of entertainment for the man who acted the presidency better than anybody else.

CHAPTER FORTY-EIGHT

The Cares of Office

FOR A MAN OF SUCH PRODIGIOUS STRENGTH, Washington had been pestered by recurrent medical problems, and his presidency proved no exception. He had weathered more than eight years of war partly because as a planter he was accustomed to a rugged outdoor life. As president, he found it hard to adapt to a sedentary job in an urban setting, which may have weakened his health. In mid-June 1789 he ran a fever as a fast-growing tumor appeared on his left thigh. The area grew so tender and inflamed that it became excruciating for him to sit. Four years earlier Washington had watched his Mount Vernon overseer, John Alton, "reduced to a mere skeleton" from a fatal abscess on his thigh, and he must have been alarmed when he developed a comparable symptom.[1]

The president summoned Dr. Samuel Bard, a prominent New York physician, who diagnosed the condition as the cutaneous form of anthrax. Petrified that Washington would expire, Bard refused to leave his bedside for several days. The situation must have shocked everyone around Washington: no sooner had the federal government been formed than its president lay in mortal peril. In all likelihood, Washington had a carbuncle or soft tissue infection. As might be expected, he was the picture of stoic courage. "I am not afraid to die and therefore can bear the worst," he told Bard evenly. "Whether tonight, or twenty years hence, makes no difference. I know that I am in the hands of a good Providence."[2] The public knew something was wrong, if only because Tobias Lear had servants cordon off Cherry Street, stopping traffic. The household staff also sprinkled straw outside the mansion to deaden passing footsteps. Still, the public had no notion of the gravity of the president's illness.

On June 17, when Dr. Bard operated on Washington's thigh, he brought along his father, Dr. John Bard, to supervise the proceedings. The elder Bard, a veteran surgeon, felt too old to undertake the procedure himself. Surgery was then a hellish ordeal, as the patient gritted his teeth and endured excruciating pain. While the younger Dr. Bard split open the abscess, his father exhorted him to persevere: "Cut away—deeper—deeper still! Don't be afraid. You see how well he bears it!"[3] Tobias Lear claimed that the tumor was "very large and the incision on opening it deep."[4] In all likelihood, the younger Bard excised the mass of infected tissue and scraped away any pus or dead tissue, all of which would have been enormously painful for Washington, who remained unfailingly courteous. As Samuel Bard assured his daughter, "It will give you pleasure to be told that nothing can exceed the kindness and attention I receive from him."[5]

For weeks afterward, as Washington lay bedridden, some friends thought he might never recover his legendary strength. "I have now the pleasure to inform you that my health is restored," Washington apprised James McHenry on July 3, "but a feebleness still hangs upon me, and I am yet much incommoded by the incision which was made in a very large and painful tumor on the protuberance of my thigh."[6] In extreme discomfort, unable to walk or sit, he reclined on his right side for six weeks and couldn't even draft a letter. When Abigail Adams visited, she found him, with becoming presidential dignity, stretched out on the sofa and praised this "singular example of modesty and diffidence."[7]

The interior of Washington's coach was reconfigured so he could lie down, although he had to be lifted and deposited gently inside by four servants. For an hour each day, he made salutary tours of the town with Martha. On July 4, 1789, Baron von Steuben and Alexander Hamilton—now, respectively, president and vice president of the New York Society of the Cincinnati—trooped to 3 Cherry Street to pay their respects before Hamilton delivered a eulogy to Nathanael Greene at St. Paul's Chapel. In a moving homage to Greene's memory, Washington, despite his discomfort, dressed up in full regimentals to greet his visitors at the door—an unusual instance of Washington donning a military costume during his presidency. To the limited extent possible, he kept up appearances and tried to convey an aura of calm.

By early September, Washington reassured Dr. James Craik that the inflammation had dwindled to "the size of a barleycorn" and that he expected it would shortly disappear altogether.[8] Martha Washington was hugely relieved, although a visitor noticed that when she discussed her husband's health, "a tear of apprehension for futurity was in her eye."[9] Except with intimates, Washington was discreet about discussing his malady. Dr. Craik and other friends urged him to launch a brisk regimen of outdoor exercise to offset his staid indoor life. Washington conceded that his job might have contributed to his ailment and might even kill him, but he was resigned to the sacrifice. Echoing Shakespeare, he said, "The want of regular exercise, with the cares of office, will, I have no doubt, hasten my departure for that country from whence no traveler returns."[10] Nevertheless, his official duties, he maintained, would remain "the primary consideration in every transaction of my life, be the consequences what they may."[11]

Washington took to heart his friends' advice to do more exercise, which was one reason he made a trip to New England that fall. Upon his return, he and Martha, along with Nelly and Washy, began extended coach rides around Manhattan, often cruising a fourteen-mile loop that took them to the scenic northern reaches of the island. Even in the winter, Washington supplemented these excursions with strolls around the Battery. Sometimes he mixed in a smattering of politics, as happened in January when he went horseback riding with Senator Samuel Johnston of North Carolina and William Cushing, an associate justice of the Supreme Court—a perfect equestrian union of all three branches of government.

WASHINGTON'S ILLNESS coincided with the final stages of Mary Ball Washington's protracted struggle with breast cancer. Showing belated maternal warmth, Mary had her daughter, Betty, write to the new president, apropos of his convalescence, that she "wishes to hear from you; *she will not believe you are well till she has it from under your own hand.*"[12] Mary had always been a hardy woman and, even as she aged, retained "full enjoyment of her mental faculties," according to her famous son.[13] Clinging to her independence, she still made daily visits to her farm in an open carriage, until illness rendered that impossible. When he visited his redoubtable mother in early March 1789, Washington knew he might never see her again and that it would be "the last act of *personal* duty I may . . . ever have it in my power to pay my mother."[14] It is significant that he employed the word *duty,* since affection had never formed part of the picture. Whatever she may have said privately, Mary Washington took no more public pride in his being president than she had in his command of the Continental Army. But it's hard to imagine that on his last visit to his mother, Washington was unmoved by the sight of a dying parent, cruelly disfigured by disease, or that he felt no residual gratitude toward her. Whatever her glaring flaws, Mary Washington had worked hard to raise him in the absence of a father.

By mid-August Mary Ball Washington had drifted into a coma; she finally passed away on August 25, 1789, at eighty-one. On September 1 Washington was hosting a dinner party, with Steuben keeping the table in uproarious merriment, when the laughter was abruptly silenced by a message announcing her death. Despite his reservations about his mother, Washington was much too decorous to dispense with the proper forms of mourning. Always correct in his conduct toward his mother, he ordered black cockades and ribbons for his household staff, while government members wore black crape on their arms; black ribbons and necklaces became de rigueur for ladies. Official New York went into mourning for a woman whom they had never seen and who had shown scant interest in the new government. The formal levees were canceled for three weeks. Soon the capital resumed its normal social rhythm, but Washington wore badges of mourning for at least five months. In what seems like shocking neglect, however, he failed to erect a tombstone on his mother's grave. "The grave of Washington's mother is marked by no visible object, not even a mound of earth, nor is the precise spot of its locality known," noted an astonished Jared Sparks during an 1827 visit to Fredericksburg. ". . . For a long time a single cedar tree was the only guide to the place; near this tree tradition has fixed the grave of Washington's mother, but there is no stone to point out the place."[15] No special memorial arose at Mary Washington's graveside until three decades after George Washington's death.

Washington spoke no eulogies, told no fond anecdotes of the hard, sometimes shrewish mother who had served as the lifelong whetstone of his anger; he took refuge instead in empty generalities. Whether responding to an unspoken accusation from Betty Lewis that he had been derelict in his filial duties, or feeling guilty that his sister had borne the burden of caring for their infirm mother, Washington sent her a detailed accounting of his financial generosity to their mother:

> She has had a great deal of money from me at times, as can be made [to] appear by my books and the accounts of Mr. L[und] Washington during my absence. And over and above this [she] has not only had all that was ever made from the plantation, but got her provisions and everything else she thought proper from thence. In short, to the best of my recollection, I have never in my life received a copper from the estate and have paid many hundred pounds (first and last) to her in cash. However, I want no retribution. I conceived it to be a duty whenever she asked for money and I had it to furnish her.[16]

In her will, Mary Washington named George as executor, a responsibility he couldn't have relished as president. She left him a bed, curtains, a blue and white quilt, and a dressing mirror—items he identified as "mementoes of parental affection," but he never took possession of them and left them for his sister's use.[17] Entitled to a one-fifth portion of his mother's estate, he received two slaves, which meant that Mary Ball Washington had owned as many as ten slaves, certifying that she had scarcely been destitute. The auction of Mary's belongings that October also suggested that, for all her complaints, the elderly widow had accumulated considerable property. Among the auction items cited in a newspaper advertisement were "stocks of horses, cattle, sheep and hogs, plantation utensils of every kind, carts, hay, and fodder."[18] In fact, Mary had amassed such substantial landholdings that George alone inherited four hundred acres of valuable pine land; he gave it to Robert Lewis, Betty's son. All of this property had been owned by a woman who saw fit to petition the Virginia legislature for a private pension during the war because of her son's alleged neglect.

THE MENACING GROWTH ON HIS THIGH and his mother's death slowed Washington down only slightly as he forged the office of the presidency, which immediately involved him in a thicket of constitutional issues. Could the Supreme Court give advisory opinions to the legislative and executive branches? Would the executive branch supervise American foreign policy, subject to congressional approval, or vice versa? Numberless questions about the basic nature of the federal government would be decided during Washington's presidency, often in the throes of heated controversy. Although Washington had not been an architect of the system of checks and balances or separation of powers, he gave sharp definition to them by helping to draw the boundaries of the three branches of government in a series of critical test cases.

A central component of the Whig orthodoxy that had spurred the American Revolution was the supremacy of the legislative branch, viewed as a curb to the executive. By design, the framers of the Constitution devoted Article I to a lengthy description of legislative powers, giving Congress the ability to help shape the other two branches. Left deliberately vague was the office of the presidency, allowing its first occupant to fill in the blanks. The earnest Washington tried to adhere to the letter of the Constitution and hoped to enjoy harmonious relations with Congress. But he soon realized that the Constitution was less a precise blueprint for action than a set of general guidelines whose many ambiguities required practical clarification. If bemused by some congressional practices, he tried not to trespass on legislative prerogatives. For instance, he privately opposed the Senate's closed-door policy, but he kept a discreet silence in public. For its part, Congress groped to define its relationship to the president. In June 1789 some congressmen wanted Washington to have to gain senatorial approval to fire as well as hire executive officers—the Constitution was silent on the subject; the House duly approved that crippling encroachment on executive authority. When the Senate vote ended in a tie, Vice President Adams cast the deciding vote to defeat the measure, thereby permitting the president to exert true leadership over his cabinet and, for better or worse, preventing the emergence of a parliamentary democracy.

The first formal clash between Washington and Congress arose on August 5, 1789, when the Senate rejected Washington's nomination of Benjamin Fishbourn as collector of the Port of Savannah. Though still ailing, Washington made his way to Federal Hall and mounted to the second-floor Senate chamber, decorated on its ceiling with thirteen stars and suns. Washington's unexpected entrance stunned the legislators. Undoubtedly feeling a bit befuddled, Vice President Adams rose from his canopied chair of crimson velvet and offered it to Washington, who then proceeded to upbraid the twenty-two members of the Senate, demanding to know why they had spurned his appointee. "The president showed [a] great want of temper . . . when one of his nominations was rejected," said Senator Ralph Izard of South Carolina.[19] It was an unusual public display of emotion by Washington.

After a long, awkward silence, Senator James Gunn of Georgia, whose state included Savannah, rose and from "personal respect for the personal character of Gen[era]l Washington" explained his opposition to Fishbourn.[20] At the same time he wanted it understood that the Senate felt no obligation to explain its reasoning to the president. The episode marked the start of "senatorial courtesy," whereby senators reserved the right to block nominations in their home states. Despite Gunn's respectful treatment, Washington went off in a great huff, and Tobias Lear said that as soon as he returned from the Senate, he "expressed his very great regret for having gone there."[21]

This skirmish turned out to be trifling compared to the conflict over Indian policy some weeks later. The episode began in mid-June, when Henry Knox, secretary of war, wrote a well-meaning letter to Washington, fleshing out a farsighted approach to Indian affairs. Noting the bloody battles between Indians and American settlers on the frontier, Knox declared that the Indians, as rightful owners of the land, should not be deprived of it by violence or coercion. Rather, he advocated paying them for their land and concentrating them in a system of federally protected enclaves. Knox wanted to initiate this policy by negotiating a treaty with Alexander McGillivray, chief of the Creek Nation, whose hunting grounds extended over parts of modern-day Georgia, Florida, Alabama, and Mississippi. The corrupt Georgia legislature was ready to make a mockery of any enlightened policy toward the Indians by selling to speculators millions of acres claimed by the Creeks and other southern tribes.

In early August Knox informed Washington that he had worked out a treaty with the Creeks, including several secret articles. Among other things, Knox wanted the executive branch to dominate Indian affairs as a way of bolstering presidential authority. As part of the treaty process, Washington planned to send a three-man commission to broker peace between Georgia and the Creeks, but when Knox drew up instructions for this parley, Washington thought he needed to consult the Senate about them. This time, instead of pouncing unexpectedly, he gave ample warning of his visit. He interpreted the "advice and consent" requirement of the Constitution to include such direct meetings with the Senate, but the ensuing contretemps changed the course of American history. When Washington arrived on August 22, he again occupied Adams's seat, with Knox seated to his left. They delivered a copy of the treaty papers to Adams, who tried to read them aloud but was drowned out by traffic below. "I could tell it was something about Indians," grumbled William Maclay, "but was not master of one sentence of it."[22] When the windows were shut, Adams read aloud the seven articles of the treaty, to be followed by a yea or nay vote on each. After he read the first one, Robert Morris stood and said he hadn't been able to hear anything above the racket, forcing Adams to reread the whole treaty. He then recited the first article again, followed by an uncomfortable silence.

Some in the Senate believed that Washington wanted them merely to rubber-stamp treaties and appointments instead of exercising independent judgment. When Maclay requested a reading of the supporting treaties between the southern Indians and three southern states, Washington fixed him with an icy glare. "I cast an eye at the president of the United States," Maclay wrote. "I saw he wore an aspect of stern displeasure."[23] Robert Morris moved that the papers brought by Washington be referred to a committee. When Maclay defended the propriety of this motion, Washington's expression grew even more forbidding, and he hotly contested the idea of committing anything to a committee. "'This defeats every purpose of my coming here' were the first words that he said," Maclay wrote in his diary. "He then went on that he had brought his Secretary at War with him to give every necessary information."[24] Washington refused to yield on the committee proposal, although he agreed to postpone the matter. In Maclay's version of events, Washington, having shown flashes of temper, withdrew with "a discontented air" and a sense of "sullen dignity."[25]

A couple of days later Washington returned to the Senate, which approved the three commissioners to negotiate with the Creeks. It proved his farewell appearance in the Senate chamber. In a decision pregnant with lasting consequences, Washington decided that he would henceforth communicate with that body on paper rather than in person and trim "advice and consent" to the word *consent*. For instance, when Washington appointed David Humphreys as a diplomat to the Court of Portugal in February 1791, Maclay noted that the choice was sent to the Senate as a fait accompli: "The president sends first and asks for our advice and consent after."[26]

This decision may have done more to define the presidency and the conduct of American foreign policy than an entire bookshelf of Supreme Court decisions on the separation of powers. Where the Constitution had been sketchy about presidential powers in foreign affairs, Washington made the chief executive the principal actor, enabling him to initiate treaties and nominate appointees without first huddling with the Senate. It was an instinctive reaction from a man who had grown accustomed to command during the war. If a touch imperious, it was a far more realistic approach to foreign policy than constant collaboration and horse-trading between the president and Senate. For one thing, the presidency was continuously in session, unlike Congress, and it was much easier for one man to take decisive action, especially in an emergency. Washington's decision also widened the distance between president and Senate, enabling the latter to function as an independent, critical voice in foreign policy rather than as a subordinate advisory panel.

An enduring mystery of Washington's presidency is why he relegated John Adams to a minor role. A Washington biographer is struck by the paucity of letters exchanged between the two men; Adams was clearly excluded from the inner circle of advisers. Partly this was a structural phenomenon. Under the Constitution, the vice president served as president of the Senate, thus overlapping two branches of governments. Nowadays we tend to think of the vice president as the president's agent in the legislature, but Adams saw the vice president as a creature of that branch. He stated bluntly, "The office I hold is totally detached from the executive authority and confined to the legislative."[27] On another occasion he insisted that the Constitution had created "two great offices," with one officer "placed at the head of the executive, the other at the head of the legislature."[28] As Washington tried to protect the presidency from senatorial intrusion, Adams was bound to suffer a demotion in the process.

Washington also had a long memory for wartime critics and knew that in the Congress Adams had sometimes been a vocal opponent of his performance. The Virginian demanded loyalty from those around him, and Adams had forfeited that trust during the war, never to regain it completely. An envious man, Adams was secretly exasperated by Washington's unprecedented success. Always brooding about history's judgment, he dreaded that Washington and Franklin would dwarf him in the textbooks. As he memorably told Dr. Benjamin Rush, the crux of the story would be "that Dr. Franklin's electrical rod smote the earth and out sprung General Washington. That Franklin electrified him with his rod and thenceforward these two conducted all the policy, negotiations, legislatures, and war."[29] Adams went so far as to say privately that Washington's waiving of his salary as commander in chief and retiring after the war had been egotistical acts: "In wiser and more virtuous times, he would not have [done] that, for that is an ambition."[30] There was also a profound temperamental gulf between Washington and Adams. Both were stubborn, gritty men with courageous devotion to American liberty, but Washington was far more restrained and self-effacing. It also couldn't have helped relations between the two men that Adams was an age peer and political rival to Washington, who preferred drawing on the talents of younger men, such as Madison and Hamilton. Of his time as vice president, John Adams would render a glum assessment: "My country has, in its wisdom, contrived for me the most insignificant office that ever the invention of a man contrived or his imagination conceived."[31]

to be continue...